THE BROOKSIDE FILES

THE BROOKSIDE FILES

GEOFF TIBBALLS
With a foreword by Phil Redmond

BⒺXTREE

IN ASSOCIATION WITH CHANNEL FOUR TELEVISION

First published in 1996 by Boxtree Limited

an imprint of Macmillan Publishers Ltd
25 Eccleston Place, London, SW1W 9NF
and Basingstoke

Associated companies throughout the world

ISBN 0 7522 1120 X

Text © Phil Redmond Enterprises Ltd 1996
Photographs © The Mersey Television Company Ltd 1996

1 2 3 4 5 6 7 8 9 10

A CIP catalogue entry for this book is available from the British Library.

Designed by Blackjacks
Reproduction by Scanners
Printed and bound by Redwood Books, Trowbridge, Wiltshire.

Acknowledgements:
The author and publishers would like to thank Mal Young and the staff and cast of
Brookside at Mersey Television for all their help in the preparation of this book.

CONTENTS

FOREWORD

F rom day one of Brookside back in 1982, we have hit a controversial nerve. First there were complaints about the amount of swearing, then later we covered emotive subjects like the rape of Shelia Grant and the Jordache storyline. Now, fourteen years later, people are getting worked up again, this time about the Simpsons.

There's nothing new about incest – the Greeks were writing about it centuries ago. Nor is there anything new in dramatising it. The phrase Oedipus complex comes from a Greek tragedy. We ourselves touched upon it with Trevor and Rachel Jordache. But a lot of people seem to want to keep all issues in the background, to sweep things under the carpet as if they don't exist. But they do exist and, as such, Brookside is perfectly entitled to look at them. That is one of the major strengths of the show – we explore issues that other soaps shy away from.

To be honest, a lot of the reaction to the Simpsons' storyline has been all too predictable. It's usually the same old people who complain about these things in the press and they always jump to the conclusion that the part to which they object – in this case Nat and Georgia in bed – is going to be the only one which will influence the rest of the audience. But how do they know that more people won't follow Max Farnham's line of indignant outrage at the thought of brother and sister sleeping together? But then that wouldn't fit their argument. In the end, by far the most Important reaction is that of the audience. And over seven million people have enjoyed the storyline. There have been only three complaints to the industry watchdog from viewers who said it made them feel uncomfortable.

The Simpsons' story is not just about incest. It is also about the complexities of human relationships, which is one of our recurring themes on Brookside. The aim has always been to feature stories and human beings that you recognise and know – the type of people with whom you can identify. Each character in Brookside is a human being with an imperfect but very real personality. Our viewers watch a character dealing with his or her life and they can relate to similar events in their own lives. Again, that is one of Brookside's strengths – it takes issues of the day and shows their impact on real people. Our characters are as real as the houses on the Close. We don't use cardboard characters or cardboard sets.

FOREWORD

Over the years, we've had some particularly satisfying storylines – Billy and Shelia, the Jordaches, Patricia Farnham's breast cancer, to name but a few. In that time, we have received tremendous praise from various organisations for highlighting issues within society. The British Dyslexia Association (over the Geoff Rogers storyline), the Down's Syndrome Association (Alice Farnham) and Refuge, the domestic violence charity (the Jordaches) are just some of the organisations who have told us how much Brookside has helped raise public awareness. And our current storylines, as illustrated in this new book, are as compelling as ever.

A lot of soaps don't like going over the same ground again but Brookside is quite happy to return to certain topics, as long as they are still relevant to today's society. Just because we have covered them doesn't mean they go away. That's why I constantly return to themes like school bullying, drugs, alcohol abuse and illiteracy because they are ongoing issues. Innovation is frequently a question of revisiting previous issues but addressing them in a new way.

For instance, with drugs, we didn't just want to tackle hard drugs or soft drugs again – we wanted to show the effects of steroid abuse, particularly on a family. So we see Mick Johnson's violent mood swings and how he takes everything out on his kids. We've also hinted at Bel Simpson's problems in the past with tranquillisers. As far as Jimmy Corkhill was concerned, we felt it was important to give people hope. We wanted to show that no matter how deep they sink into degradation, there can be a way out. It has to be said that there was also the consideration that he is one of our most popular characters and so we didn't want to kill him off.

One of the important things when planning ahead is to make sure the programme maintains a good balance. Everybody has been focusing on the Simpson's lately, but there have been other good storylines, such as Sammy leaving her little daughter to go off on holiday and, on a lighter note, Sinbad and his women. Similarly, we aim to keep the right balance of characters – a good mix of social and age groups. We've always realised the importance of young characters on Brookside – it's a tradition which dates back to Damon Grant – and school invariably plays a major part because, at that age, it's woven into your life. And in David Crosbie, we've got an extremely vocal representative of the older generation.

When I created Brookside, I brought to it some of the lessons I'd learned from Grange Hill. The essential factor for the success of a programme like ours is to keep up to date with the audience. If we do that and keep revisiting the vital issues of the day, there's no reason why we can't take the residents of Brookside Close well into the 21st century.

RHIL REDMOND

CRIME

Jimmy Corkhill on Drugs

Jimmy Corkhill had always sailed close to the wind. There were scams, knock-off gear and even driving the getaway car on an armed robbery where he exacted a full and bloody revenge on his old enemy, Joey Godden. But when Jimmy first got involved in drugs in the summer of 1993, his past crimes paled into insignificance. As first an addict, then a pusher, Jimmy became Brookside's public enemy number one.

It all started when I was working at La Luz. I caught a couple of kids in the bog with some funny-looking pills. As head of security, I was in a position of responsibility, like, so I grabbed them off 'em. The next night, I showed the pills to that ponce Brian Kennedy who ran the hair salon and he kept on at me to take one. He said they were E – Ecstasy. Now I may have wandered from the straight and narrow a bit in the past but I'd never taken drugs. And I didn't want to start then. But he was basically calling me chicken...and no one calls a Corkhill chicken. So I slipped one down with me pint and before I knew it I was on the dance floor making John

Brookside's series producer Mal Young: 'At the time we were planning this storyline, all the anti-drugs campaigns appeared to be targeting youngsters, not people Jimmy's age. At Brookside we sometimes like to put a different slant on things so we decided to take this guy who'd just got into his 40s and had never touched drugs in his life and we knew that in a year or two's time, we'd have him completely destroyed and also destroying other families like the Dixons. We gave him everything – when it looked like drugs were the answer – then took it away from him. Jimmy's story was always designed to be a three-to-four-year story and it's fair to say that in the middle parts, the audience were getting a bit frustrated, wanting to know when he was going to get his comeuppance. We started reading letters in magazines accusing us of supporting drugs because we were allowing Jimmy to get away with things, but we said: "Don't judge us yet. It's a long story." And eventually we even began to get favourable letters from parents who thanked us for introducing the subject and said they were able to talk to their own children and identify with the problems of drugs via the show. It's great that people want to use a drama in that way. We're not offering the answers – we're just providing a platform maybe for them to find their own answers.'

CRIME

Travolta look like Douglas Bader. I was well out of it. Barry Grant went spare, dealing going on in his club, but Brian told me he'd been offered something in La Luz only the week before.

'He said he had lots of mates who liked to pop a pill or something to liven up their night out. He said I should supply them with the stuff they wanted. If I didn't, others would. He said I could make a lot of money out of it.

'It was the pound signs flashing before me eyes that did it. I'd always wanted to make big money, just so as I could repay Jackie for sticking by me. I could buy her the dream house that she's always wanted. I was still a bit reluctant – to me, druggies were losers – but Brian said he took drugs and he looked all right to me. I mean, he was a successful businessman. He wore a suit. And none of our family ever wore a suit unless they were in court. Brian was right, it was easy money. The deals were done through the cab drivers outside the club. In a couple of months, I'd made over a grand – enough for a deposit on a house. Then Brian told me about a big shipment of cocaine coming in from abroad at the end of the week. It was out of my league but he said that if I put in just three grand, I could make five times that amount. Fifteen grand. It was too good an opportunity to miss. I was desperate to raise the cash in time. In the end, I had to hock Jackie's charm bracelet and two life insurance policies. I wasn't proud of what I was doing but I convinced meself that I was doing it for Jackie.

'I was bottling it waiting for the deal to go through. Brian suggested I try some of the stuff that was going to make my fortune. So I had me first snort of cocaine. Afterwards, I felt great, super-confident. It made me feel I could handle anything. I was in the big time and enjoying it. But fate has a nasty habit of kicking us Corkhills when we least expect it.

'Next day, as arranged, Brian turned up with a parcel all right, but instead of it containing fifteen grand in cash, there was just a bag of coke. He told me I'd got to flog it meself – I was on me own. He'd stitched me up good and proper. Jackie was doing her nut about her bracelet. She threatened to kick me out. I tried to sell the coke back to Brian – forget about any profit – but before I had a chance, he was lifted at the salon by the bizzies. I came out in a cold sweat. Brian had said I'd get ten years if I was caught. I was in it up to me neck.

I needed something to calm me down, but I ended up wrecking two families.

Poor Frank Rogers. His wedding day was destroyed by a crazed druggie – me!

'I drove straight home, me mind racing, stuffed the coke in me jacket and told Jackie I was doing a runner. As I got in the car again, the sweat was pouring off me. Driving along, I could hardly see where I was going. I needed something to calm me down. I was out of ciggies, all I had was the fifteen grand's worth of coke, so I decided a quick snort would do the trick. I hadn't got time to stop. With one hand on the wheel, I piled some coke on to a scrap of old card and turned away to get the stuff up me nose. Instant relief. But when I turned back, I suddenly saw this white Roller – a wedding car – heading straight for me. I realised I was on the wrong side of the road and swerved. The roller went the other way...straight into a brick wall. With ten years hanging over me, I knew I couldn't stop. I just carried on to La Luz

and stashed the coke in the toilet. With it safely hidden away, I began to breathe a little easier. The club was all laid out for Frank Rogers' wedding reception. Then the news came through that the wedding car had crashed. Frank was dead, and young Tony Dixon was in a coma. It was all down to me. I had never felt so low.

'Through work, I was able to keep me head down for a while out in Spain until I thought it was safe to come back. I was just praying that Tony Dixon hadn't died. I had a lot of explaining to do to Jackie but I fobbed her off with some story about a business deal going wrong. She wasn't impressed, but I knew she'd come round in the

CRIME

end. She always did. And she was still going on about that bracelet of hers. I explained that I'd get it back as soon as I could, but in the meantime she said if I really wanted to get in her good books, I could go with her to visit Tony Dixon in hospital. My heart sank. Worse still, when we got there Ron had just been told that it was highly unlikely that Tony would ever come round. I was racked with guilt. Thank God nobody knew. At that point, I would have done anything to turn back the clock, so when Ron said something about there being places in America which might be able to help their Tony, I immediately appointed meself as his official fund-raiser. It was the least I could do. Jackie was so touched she allowed me back home. If only I could've told her...

'The nightmares about Tony grew worse. Taking coke was the only thing that stopped them doing me head in. Soon I'd got through the whole three grand. I used to take it in the bathroom, in front of the mirror, but one day Jackie caught me. Shocked, she snatched it out of me hand and flushed it down the loo – twenty quid's worth. I pushed her out and locked the door, and sat in the corner with me hands over me ears to drown out her banging and shouting. She said

I put Ron Dixon through hell – no wonder he hates me.

something about me not needing to take drugs – think of poor Ron Dixon. It was then that I blurted out that it was me who killed Frank Rogers and put Tony in a coma. It was such a relief to get it off me chest at last. Jackie never told anyone.

'When Tony finally died, the shock hit me like a hammer blow. To make things worse, Ron asked me if I'd be a coffin bearer because of me fund-raising. I could hardly live with meself. I needed something to get me through it. That's when I had

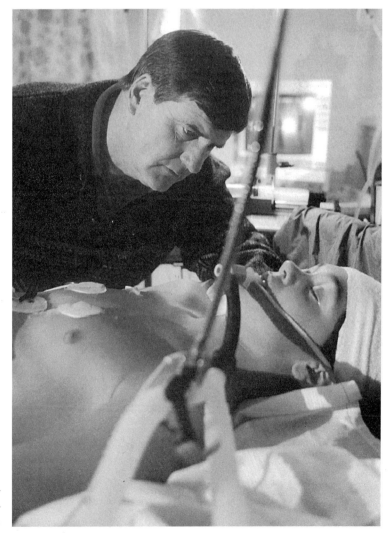

me first hit of smack, heroin. I told Jackie I wasn't an addict – I could stop whenever I wanted. It's just that I didn't want to. She had arranged for me wages at the club to be paid direct to her, to stop me spending them on drugs. She gave me a bit of pocket money each week. It was so humiliating. I felt like a little kid, being given a pat on the head and told to run along and buy some sweets. In a moment of despair, I told the bizzies about the crash. They said I'd be charged with failing to report an accident. Ron Dixon found out and followed me to some smack-house. I had a bad hit there and Ron could have left me to die. He was probably tempted. I could hardly blame him. I woke up in hospital.

'I did me best to get off drugs – I even saw some counsellor – but, looking back, I was too far gone, I was hooked. And it was doing me head in not having enough money for a daily fix. So I went back on the rob. I started nicking things from tills, then moved on to burglary. First Oscar Dean, who co-owned La Luz – he was away in Spain at the time – then closer to home, at the Farnhams' house. I never did have any time for Max Farnham   he was always looking down at me. Toffee-nosed git! By now, the whole Close knew about me drug problem so I was the prime suspect, like. I had to use all the old Jimmy Corkhill charm to protest me innocence. When Jackie found me with a pocket full of readies, I thought me number was up, but I managed to persuade her that the money was to get her charm bracelet back. She was well pleased. But then I pushed me luck, robbing the new family on

the Close. Eddie Banks caught me red-handed. He was a big burly bloke and there was no escape. Next thing I knew I'd got nine months in Walton.

'Prison was hell at first. I missed Jackie like mad. I had this Scottish cellmate, Don Macatyre, seemed a right hard case, the sort who was probably better looking in a stocking mask. But we had more in common than I thought. He had a supply of smack stored on the inside of an extractor fan in the kitchens, a place where the screws never looked. One night, he was well gone. I told him to slow down a bit, but he wouldn't listen. When the screws came to wake him in the norming, he was dead. I had to see Jackie, what had happened to Don was too close

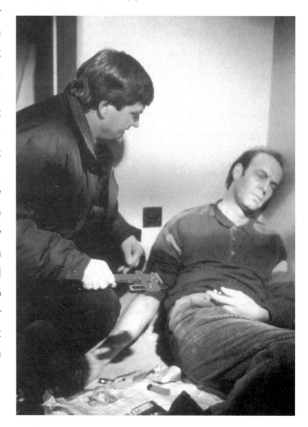

After all I'd done I wouldn't have blamed Ron if he'd left me to die.

CRIME

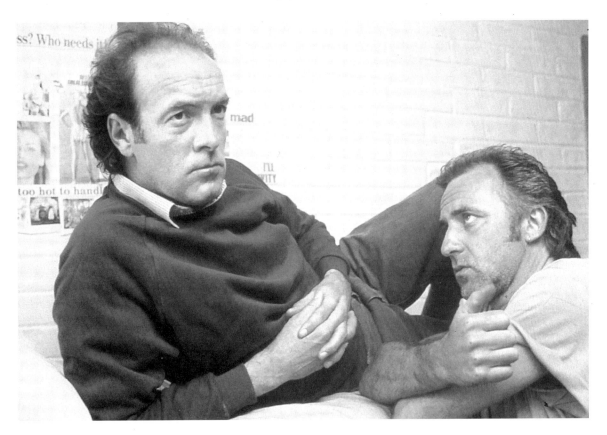

to home, it could've been me. I said I was clean and was going to stay clean. And this time I meant it. Poor Jackie was broke, behind with the rent. She needed money. And I knew where I could get me hands on plenty. The screws hadn't found Don's stash, but taking drugs was a mug's game. Dealing was where the money was.

'So when I got out, I set up in business full-time. It was so easy. Course, Jackie was still suspicious as to where the money was coming from but I swore to her that it wasn't drugs money. I was able to start up me own taxi firm, Korky Kars, as a cover for the drugs dealing. I even took on a couple of the drivers who'd been involved in dealing at the nightclub. I wasn't proud of meself for lying to her, but it was the only way I

This Don fella, who I was banged up with, showed me how to make big money.

knew of making enough money to buy her that dream house. And when I'd saved up enough to buy the Jordaches' old place, you should have seen her face. It was a picture. And I even had enough left for a new patio. Back with me wife, house of me own, plenty of readies. Who says Jimmy Corkhill's a loser?

'Korky Kars, but especially its subsidiary, was a thriving concern. If it had been legit, I reckon I could've been up for Merseyside Businessman of the Year. I was even able to look at meself in the mirror. Then our Lindsey turned up on the doorstep out of the blue, saying she'd left that no-mark

husband of hers, Gary. I never have liked Gary – he's a lazy pillock, a complete waste of space. And I won't have anyone upsetting my little girl. Soon he turned up, begging for Lindsey to go back to him and promising to get a job. She wanted to give him another chance so against me better judgement, I offered him a job as a taxi driver.

'You'd think he'd have been grateful that I'd given him a job when nobody else in their right mind would, but soon the greedy little sod was

CRIME

Me business premises offered the perfect cover for me drug-dealing operations.

'It would've broken our Lindsey's heart – I was her dad. Besides, I thought even Gary couldn't muck up delivering a few packages. But he only went and got himself followed by the bizzies. Early one morning, they came and smashed the door down and there were sniffer dogs all over me shag-pile. Jackie thought I was up to me old tricks. But I managed to convince her I was an innocent victim of police harassment. I was so good I started to believe it meself. Anyway after a visit from the boys in blue, me regular supplier pulled out. Gary, full of big ideas as usual, said forget about the middle man, why don't we get the gear ourselves? I thought he should learn to walk before he could run.

'Then just before Christmas it all blew up in me face. Jackie went nosing around me lock-up and found me stash of drugs. She went ballistic. She started screaming that she wanted nothing to do with anything that had been bought with drug money. I said that included the house, all the furnishings, all her fancy clothes. Did she want to go back to the old days of scrimping and saving? She said she was going to leave me, but I hoped she wouldn't. You see, deep down Jackie's the same as me – she's always wanted to better herself. Now for the first time in her life she had the good things in life. It made her feel good. I knew she couldn't give it up. And let's face it, if blokes didn't buy their drugs off me, they'd only get 'em somewhere else.

'Gary fixed us up with some supplier in Holland and I was able to undercut the local heroin

poking his nose into me affairs. He wanted in on the operation, threatening to expose me to Lindsey if I didn't cut him in. It was nothing short of blackmail. But I couldn't risk Lindsey and Jackie finding out about me little sideline.

dealers by five per cent. Business was booming. Soon I'd be able to buy the whole Close.

'But one of the Liverpool mafia, Big Davey, wasn't too pleased and put a bullet through our window and we had the police all over our house again. Jackie told Lindsey all about me and drugs. She was horrified. The shooting was the last straw for Jackie and Lindsey and they packed their bags. What if little Kylie had been hit? they said. I pleaded with Jackie to stay, but she wouldn't unless I promised to stop dealing. I wanted to say I'd stop, but I couldn't. I just couldn't. I watched the three people I loved most in life walk out the door. I realised I'd lost everything...and all because of drugs.

'I decided to stop there and then, but Gary was all for selling the stuff we'd got. Unknown to me, the dickhead flogged some uncut heroin to that Aussie soap star, Shane Cochran. We tried to warn Shane but we got to the theatre where he was in a panto too late. We found him dead in his dressing-room. Now I had another death on my conscience. It really cut me up. When we got back to the Close, someone sprayed 'Jimmy Corkhill murderer – Drug dealer' on the front of the house. Jacqui Dixon, Shane's girlfriend, started sabotaging me taxi business, but I didn't care. After what I'd done to her family over the years, I deserved whatever I got.

'But you see I still hadn't really been punished. Gary made sure I was when he planted a bag of smack in Kylie's teddy

bear as Lindsey and Mike Dixon headed off to make a new life together in Australia. When I found out that my daughter and granddaughter were being held in a dirty Bangkok prison because of that little creep, I nearly killed him with me bare hands. I got him to go to the bizzies and confess but then he went and did a runner. Thank God, we finally managed to get Kylie and Lindsey out, but I tell you, I've learned me lesson. That's why I've been helping out at drugs centres and that, passing on the benefit of my experience to other addicts. I'm a reformed character, me. I'm never gong to touch drugs again – honest. And that's not a word you usually associate with the Corkhills.'

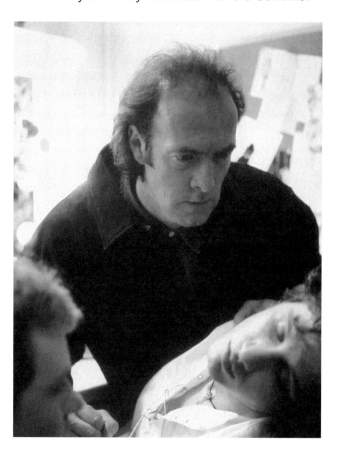

That no-mark Gary flogged the wrong stuff to Shane Cochran.

CRIME

Max Farnham on Kerb-Crawling

Max Farnham was on cloud nine. Grants had just been voted Best Restaurant on Merseyside by Mersey Nite Out, even though the piece did compare him to Basil Fawlty. But then a chance encounter with a prostitute hit business and resulted in the breakdown of his marriage.

'It was all so silly. I'd had to borrow Ron Dixon's car to get to an important radio interview. I was cutting it a bit fine anyway, but, to top it all, I got lost in a new one-way system. You know what those things are like – I could have ended up half-way to Manchester before I'd realised my mistake. So I thought I'd better ask for directions. I saw this girl – well woman really – standing on the street corner, presumably waiting for a taxi or something. She looked as if she knew her way around – that is to say, she looked as if she knew the area – so I slowed down and called over to her. Although she was a bit scantily dressed for February, it didn't occur to me for one minute that she was a prostitute, but the next thing I knew she was

B K 43 75862 02 26 96
MERSEY POLICE   MF

reeling off her price list. In the past, some people have accused me of being a little slow on the uptake but I soon cottoned on to what was going on here. I'm all for a high-celebrity profile, but I didn't want Hugh Grant's! So I explained that she misunderstood my intentions, that I was a happily married man and I made my excuses and left.

'I thought nothing more about it until Ron and Bev came in to Grants for a celebration dinner a couple of nights later. It was bad enough having them there anyway. The way Ron slurps his soup and Bev asks for ketchup on her duck à l'orange is enough to put anyone off their food. On this particular occasion, they were nearing the end of a typically sumptuous repast when Ron called me

Mal Young: 'The storyline when Max was charged with kerb-crawling originated at a time when we'd seen a number of high-profile cases in the news about men being put on trial for sex crimes of which they were subsequently proved to have been innocent. We wanted to look at how society can be influenced by the media, even before a case has gone to court. Dramas have always looked at women and how they're treated after rape, but we wanted to say: "What if a guy hadn't done something and it was someone the audience actually like?" The audience and Max were the only ones who knew he was innocent and we let them share in his frustrations, because, let's face it, we all say: "There's no smoke without fire." It worked well. There was enormous sympathy for Max and it provided us with the opportunity to work Susannah back into his affections.'

over to tell me that he had received a letter from the police, asking him to go into the station. When he got there they said that his car had been spotted in a red-light district and that he was being accused of kerb-crawling. Of course, Ron and Bev had worked out that the incident in question had taken place while I had borrowed his car. I explained that it was all a ghastly misunderstanding but, since it wasn't the sort of thing I wanted to be made public, I tried to buy their silence by saying that the meal was on the house. That really hurt, I can tell you.

'Ron and I duly went down to the station to try and sort it out. Ron was cleared, but I was given a caution. I was most indignant. And it didn't help afterwards when Ron kept going on about my name now being on police files and that if there

Me, a kerb-crawler? How ridiculous

was a rape or any major sex crime, the police would probably come knocking on my door. He reckoned the only solution was to find the girl and clear my name. So I told Patricia I had to work at the restaurant on my night off – I didn't want to worry her at that stage – and went back to find the girl. To my amazement, she said she wouldn't talk to me unless I paid her. She said she vaguely remembered me but flatly refused to go to the police on my behalf. Naively perhaps with hindsight, I offered her more money, at which point the police, who were clamping down on prostitution in the area, arrested me for soliciting. There was no caution this time, this one would be going all the way to trial.

CRIME

I couldn't believe it when the police arrested me. I was innocent for God's sake.

Patricia wouldn't stand by me over the sorry episode.

'I just couldn't bring myself to tell Patricia. I knew she'd hit the roof. I lied and told her that I'd been with Susannah, helping to sort out a little problem. True to form, Patricia wasn't pleased. She threatened to phone Susannah to give her a piece of her mind and I was terrified that Susannah would say I hadn't been round there at all, and then Patricia would think the worst, possibly that I'd been with another woman, not Susannah, which I had been, but not in the way she meant. God, it was a mess! So I rushed round to Susannah's and told her all about the misunderstanding with the prostitute and the police. She believed me, bless her, but told me to go straight home and tell Patricia the truth...before someone else did.

'I tried to tell Patricia, I really did, but somehow the words never came out. And then David, Patricia's father, showed her a newspaper with the story about the restaurateur and the prostitute. She was livid. I protested my innocence, but she just wouldn't believe me. She said if nothing happened, why hadn't I told her about it? In her mind, silence equalled guilt. And that made me angry too. She should have at least given me the benefit of the doubt. It's not as if I made a habit of visiting prostitutes. But she was acting as judge, jury and executioner. She said she wanted me out of the house, but I dug my heels in. I wasn't going anywhere.

'I slept in the spare room while Patricia continued to belittle me. She told me she could never trust me again and even insisted that I take an AIDS test before she allowed me anywhere near her or the children. It was getting ridiculous. She even took great delight in informing me that the newspaper had pulled my regular gourmet column.

'But I think what really did it was Susannah turning up on our doorstep to plead my case. Patricia had always seen Susannah as a threat – all the more so after that regrettable lapse on my part a couple of years back when, during a rough patch in our marriage, I sought solace in Susannah's arms – and now she was appalled to learn that Susannah had known all about the saga of the prostitute before she had. I can understand Patricia being hurt, but it's just that Susannah was so much easier to talk to. My wife didn't understand me, but my ex-wife did! I'm afraid I let it all get to me when I returned home to find a party in full swing next door. When I saw my father-in-law drunk as a skunk and with fluorescent orange hair, I made rather a spectacle of myself by marching in and turning the music down. And everyone just stood there, sniggering at me, making crude remarks at my expense. It was so humiliating.

'When I got the date of the court case, I was filled with dread. I thought, what chance have I got of convincing three po-faced magistrates that I'm innocent if I can't even convince my own wife? I asked Patricia whether she would at least support me in court, but she wouldn't even do that for me. I felt badly let down. Not only that, but she said she wouldn't even be around for the case – she was going to France to see her mother Jean. Whatever happened to stand by your man?

David's orange hair obviously proved a hit with Rachel Jordache but that party was a night I'd prefer to forget.

'As you know, I was found not guilty – and rightly so. But the fact that Susannah had taken the trouble to support me in court when my wife hadn't, still hurt me deeply. I didn't feel much like celebrating. When I got home, I was amazed to find Patricia there. She congratulated me but it had such a hollow ring that I packed my bags and stormed off to Susannah's. It was the only place I knew where I could find a sympathetic ear. I really didn't want to lose Patricia for good – I tried to persuade her just to go back to France for a break, see how things worked out – but it seemed that she had made up her mind. Right up to the last moment, I thought there was a chance of a reconciliation, but then she saw Susannah and a removal lorry, put two and two together and made five, and drove off with Thomas and Alice. Timing never was Susannah's strong point. Then again, the way things have turned out, perhaps it was for the best after all.'

THE BROOKSIDE FILES

Rachel Jordache on Murder and Family Loyalties

Rachel Jordache's world turned upside down when she discovered that her mother, Mandy, and elder sister Beth had killed her father Trevor. Here she talks about her confused reaction to the news and how she eventually came to the right decision in court.

'I was so thrilled when my dad came home, and I just couldn't understand why mum and Beth weren't as pleased to see him as I was. I knew something was up because they were always whispering in corners and suddenly changing the subject whenever I walked in the room. Then they said he'd gone away again. It didn't make sense – he hadn't even said goodbye. And the next thing I heard he'd been found dead somewhere. It was all a bit sketchy but mum identified the body so that was it. Even so, it was only me and Auntie Brenna who seemed to be mourning him.

'Then one afternoon, I found mum and Beth waiting to collect me from school. They muttered some garbled story and said we were all going to Ireland. I'd arranged a surprise party for Sinbad, but he ended up coming to Ireland too. It certainly wasn't my idea of a holiday. I hated every minute

Mal Young: 'With the Jordaches, Phil Redmond probably came up with the biggest storyline in soap history. Even though it was controlled by us, it took on a life of its own. The response was amazing. We had helplines for domestic violence and for child abuse, which was a separate issue. A lot of abused kids wrote in, drawing parallels with their own lives, and those letters really took my breath away. We took pains not to sensationalise either the abuse or the domestic violence on screen – we filmed them as coldly and as blandly as possible. When Beth discovered Trevor in bed with Rachel, we knew that because we went out at 5pm on a Saturday, when children were likely to be watching alone, we couldn't portray the abuse visually. We showed Trevor cuddling Rachel, which could be construed as innocent, and then getting into bed with her, but the only real indication was the look on Beth's face. In the weekday version, viewers saw Trevor's bare arm outside the bed, implying that he'd taken his clothes off, but that shot was cut for the Saturday omnibus. In effect, it proved just as powerful because it left more to the imagination. Throughout the whole Jordache storyline, we were very careful never to show a punch connect with Mandy. The violence had to be implied. You never saw the knife go in, you never saw any blood on the knife. You saw one brief shot of the knife being dropped and that's what the ITC objected to because you're not supposed to show domestic implements as weapons before the 9pm watershed. But we felt we were justified. Mandy wouldn't have had a machine gun lying around the house – she'd have used a kitchen knife. The Rachel story is by no means closed. We don't believe in neat little endings on Brookside. We want to look at her in the future and see how she's coping as a once-abused child because it is something which will be with her for the rest of her life.'

CRIME

of it and just wanted to go home. We booked in at this crumby B & B and mum, Beth and Sinbad were behaving really strange. They seemed obsessed with the papers. Then mum sat me down and blurted out that she had killed my dad. I couldn't believe what I was hearing. I shot out of that place as fast as I could. My head was spinning. I just ran – anywhere at first, just as long as it was far away from mum, Beth and Sinbad – and then I decided to go back to England. I got to the ferry terminal but one of the guards picked me up. I was taken to a police station and the three of them came to collect me.

'All I wanted to know was: why? Why had mum killed my dad? They kept coming up with these terrible stories about him touching me, but it was rubbish. My dad would never have hurt me – he

I was so confused I didn't know whether to be relieved or sad when the Irish guards found me.

loved me. He told me he loved me. Anyway, a promise is a promise...

'We went on the run, from one guest house to the next, until finally the police caught up with us. I was glad it was all over. When we got back to Liverpool, I just wanted to shut mum, Beth and Sinbad out of my life for good. I couldn't forgive them for what they had done. David and Jean Crosbie took me in. They were kind, and they didn't keep going on about the court case all the time. I remember my 16th birthday, which was more than mum did. At least I got a card from Auntie Brenna with £20 in it. Mum, who was on bail, tried to make it up to me by throwing a surprise party. It was a surprise all right. She told me she was pregnant. It was all too much for me. I flipped, and lashed out at her. It seemed that no sooner had she killed my dad than she was expecting Sinbad's baby. I couldn't help wondering whether this was why she had killed dad – that it had nothing to do with all those stories of her being beaten up, but it was just so she could get together with Sinbad. As for Beth, I thought she simply had it in for all men. I hated them both.

'I was really mixed up. I'd packed in school and to make things worse, my friend Garry Salter had drowned at the local swimming pool. It couldn't have come at a worse time – I needed all the friends I could get. Why was all this happening to me?

'At the trial, I was called as a witness for the prosecution. I was told that I just had to tell the truth. I had convinced myself that I was. The courtroom was a horrible place – cold and frightening – and my nerves were on edge. I don't think I could have got through it but for David and Jean. I did break down at one point when the defence barrister went on at me about my dad abusing me. I just didn't want to hear it. I said he used to get into bed with me to keep warm, that's all. I was so angry and confused.

'I suppose, deep down, I wanted mum and Beth to get off, even though I gave evidence against them. When they were found guilty and the judge said they were going to prison, I was stunned. It was then that it really hit me – what I'd done to them. My mum and my sister were both going to prison and it was all my fault. Auntie Brenna was gloating. It was horrible. I was meant to be going to Ireland to live with her until I found

out that it was her who had been sending mum and Beth hate mail. I suddenly saw Brenna in a different light. She was bitter and twisted, and I didn't want to end up like her. So I decided to stay with the Crosbies.

'Although I felt sorry for mum and Beth, I couldn't bring myself to visit them in prison. I knew that I'd lied in court, but they still shouldn't have killed my dad. There must have been some other way. He wasn't all bad. I know now that what he did to me was wrong, but at the time it made me feel special – like I was the one he loved best.

'But the guilt was beginning to get me down. If only there was someone I could have talked to. But everyone on the Close seemed so preoccupied with the campaign to free mum and Beth that they didn't appear to have any time for me. The only people I could trust were David and Jean, but even then I kept backing off when they got too close. I desperately wanted to tell them about the little secret dad had made me promise never to reveal, but I just couldn't. It was too private, too personal. And it would have been going back on my word to dad. Besides, if I admitted that I hadn't told the truth in court, I thought I'd be in trouble for perjury or something. I might've ended up in jail too. I didn't know what to do for the best.

'In the end, the decision was made for me. I accidentally left my bag on the bus and when it was returned David found my folder containing all the letters from dad, the ones with details of our secrets. When I discovered that him and Jean had read them, I went mad and tried to burn them in the garden. But Jean said that the letters were all I had left of my dad. That made me think.

CRIME

I couldn't destroy them – it would have been like destroying him again. I locked myself away in my room to give myself time to think. The lies had gone on long enough. I'd finally got the courage and been to see mum in jail but now they were moving her to Yorkshire. It seemed so far away. I couldn't let her continue to rot in some prison,

---

Beth was brilliant in court, but my evidence helped to send her to jail.

not when I had the key to her freedom. So I handed over the letters.

'Then just before the appeal, we heard that Beth was dead. Her heart failed. Just like that. She was gone. Mum was devastated and it made me more determined than ever to go through with it. I'd lost two of the people I loved the most, I couldn't bear to lose a third. The court seemed to be full of psychiatrists this time. I was terrified going into the witness box again, but this time I admitted what my dad had done to me. Mum was

We were all stunned when Beth died but it convinced me I had to tell the truth in court.

freed. I was pleased for her, but we were both still too shaken by what had happened to Beth. It was such a terrible waste of a young life. I know we used to row like all sisters but she had everything – brains, looks, the lot. And I miss her like crazy. But I know she'd have wanted me to get on with my life, so that's what I'm trying to do. But sometimes, after what I've been through, it's not easy.'

FAMILIES

Sammy Daniels on Leaving Daughter Louise Home Alone

Sammy Daniels' life has been an emotional roller-coaster. Her mum, Chrissy, left home on Sammy's wedding day and father Frank was killed on his wedding day. A teenage alcoholic who initially rejected baby Louise, she seemed to have settled down to married life with the steady Owen, but last spring the two separated. Rather than face the realities of life as a single parent, Sammy once more turned to the demon drink. She proceeded to seduce Max Farnham, later lying to him that she was expecting his baby. In fact, she wasn't pregnant at all — she just saw it as a way of trying to keep hold of Max. Her behaviour meant that she had run out of friends. And no friends meant no baby-sitters, presenting Sammy with a new problem.

'I get sick of everyone having a go at me. Our Katie, Jacqui Dixon, that mouthy madam Bev – all going on about me drinking too much and being a lousy mother to Louise. From the way they talk, you'd think they were paragons of virtue. But what about Katie getting involved with

that religious nutter Simon and all the trouble that followed? And Jacqui Dixon's been putting it about for years. They call her Camelot – every week a rollover. And Bev's nothing but a gold-digger. It's not fair. I just want to have a bit of fun. That's not too much to ask, is it, not with the

Mal Young: 'Some people were surprised when Sammy Daniels suddenly came back to the Close but unless we kill a character off, we always leave it wide open for them to return. In reality, people do drift in and out of other people's lives. We waited until Sammy's sister, Katie, needed someone, which was at the end of the bulimia story. To go through the bulimia episodes, Katie had to be unsupported. With Sammy, we wanted to look seriously at the plight of single mums. The "home alone" story is one which we've discussed in the past, but it's never felt right. You can't tag issues on to characters – they must come naturally. But when Sammy returned to the Close, we thought: "This girl's going to abandon her child and go off on holiday with the first fella she meets." So the story came from within the character and is therefore all the more believable. We had Bing support her, which was a surprise. You'd think he would be against single mothers but he saw her in a different light when he realised that she was trapped in a vicious circle.'

THE BROOKSIDE FILES

lousy life I've had so far? Me dad's dead, me mum's gone off to Japan and me husband's walked out on me. What have I done to deserve all that? It really gets me when I see people like Jacqui Dixon for whom everything just seems to fall into place. Why can't something good happen to me for a change?

'Things started looking up when Terry Sullivan gave me a job at La Luz, but then came the business with Max. I know I was silly, but I fancied him rotten. At the time, I needed a man. When all that blew up in me face, I suppose I started drinking again. Anyway, there's nothing wrong with having a drink or two, especially if some dishy fella's buying. I always used to manage to

Max Farnham used me and then treated me like dirt. So I decided to get me own back.

find someone to look after Louise while I was at work but after a bit, none of me so-called mates would baby-sit for me. Katie had rehearsals for some crappy dance show, Rachel was off visiting her mad mother down in Bristol and Jacqui didn't want to know anyway. She only ever thinks of herself. So I had no choice but to take Louise into the club and let her sleep in the office while I served behind the bar. It wasn't the perfect arrangement, but it seemed OK to me. But then Mo told me Terry had heard about me bringing Louise in and was on the warpath. Apparently, he

FAMILIES

reckoned a four-year-old was under age at La Luz – judging by some of the clientele I've seen in there, only just.

'So I quickly took Louise home, tucked her into bed and left her a sandwich and a glass of milk and the number of the club if she got worried. When I got back to the club, Mo started giving me the third degree about what I'd done with my daughter. She was ranting and raving about me leaving a young kid in the house on her own, but it was none of her business.

'Louise didn't mind staying at home and it gave me a bit of freedom – the chance to meet a decent bloke. One night I met this fella called Noel and we went home for a coffee. I could tell he really fancied me – he was making all the right moves – but just as we were about to get down to it, Louise ruined everything with her crying. She'd had a bad dream. By the time I'd put her back to bed, Noel had done a runner. I was really fed up. Having a kid was cramping me style.

'Luckily Noel came back to the club a couple of nights later. This time, I decided to tell him that Louise wasn't my baby at all, but my sister's. It did the trick. We got on like a house on fire. I was going to tell him the truth eventually – I just wanted to get to know him better first. He was really great – I thought he was definitely the one for me – so when he said he'd got cheap last-minute tickets for a package holiday in Tenerife and wanted me to go with him, I jumped at the chance. It was ages since I'd had a decent holiday. I think I deserved one, don't you?

'Terry let me have the time off and I was sure Katie would look after Louise. I even made her a special meal as a thank you. I wanted to wait for her to get back from rehearsals to explain where I was going, but Noel had got a cab. The meter was ticking away, and anyway we might have missed the plane if we'd hung around any longer. I rang Katie at the theatre but she'd already left. It usually only takes her fifteen minutes to get home, so I thought Louise would

Noel's offer of a holiday in Tenerife was too good to refuse.

easily be all right for that long, until her Auntie Katie got home. After all, I'd left her for longer than that before, hadn't I? I left Katie a note. I wasn't to know she'd be dashing straight off to some poxy hairdressing show in Birmingham without even reading it.

'I had a fantastic holiday – but what a welcome back. No sooner had we touched down than the police were waiting to arrest me at the airport. They said something about Louise having been taken into care by the Social Services, but I didn't really understand what they were going on about. I was still tired from the flight. Later they

I'd had a great holiday, only to find the police waiting for me at the airport.

told me I was being charged with wilful neglect or something.

'This stupid solicitor suggested I should plead guilty to show how sorry I was for what had happened, that way the court might let me off lightly, but why should I? I hadn't done nothing wrong. I'm entitled to a life, aren't I? I'd done me best to make sure Louise would be looked after while I was away. It wasn't my fault it had all gone wrong. That was down to Katie. She should have been more responsible. Worse still, Noel didn't want to know any more. Don't people realise how hard it is for a single mum to meet anyone?

'I could feel everyone whispering behind me back, except for Jacqui Dixon and Bev, they just come straight out and say it to your face. Talk

FAMILIES

Bel Simpson should have minded her own business.

about kicking someone when they're down. And if it hadn't been for Bel Simpson sticking her nose in, calling the Social Services while I was in Tenerife, none of this would have happened. And there was loads of stuff about me in the papers. People who didn't even know me were slagging me off. It was all so unfair. Why does it always happen to me? Why is my life such a mess?

'I had to go to this case conference so that I could try and get Louise back. These snooty social workers started asking me about the time I'd left Louise as a baby, but that was different. They wanted to know whether Owen or his family would help, so I told them the truth about Louise's precious father, how he'd met someone else and gone off and left me and his daughter in the lurch. I didn't want anything from the Daniels family.

'They said I could have Louise back if I made proper childcare arrangements. I just wanted her back whatever, but my wages from the club didn't leave me with enough to pay for a childminder. Terry said he couldn't give me a rise, so I decided

the only solution was for him to pay me cash in hand and for me to claim dole money. Fee Phelan also gave me a job, helping out in the beauty salon. Course, interfering know-alls like Jacqui and Julia Brogan were quick to call me a scrounger, but I wasn't doing it for me, I was doing it for Louise. I was trying to be a good mother. It was her first day at school and I felt really guilty about not being able to afford to buy her a new winter coat. With a bit of money in me hand, I'd be able to change all that. But nobody understood.

'The one person who really came through for me was David Crosbie. I'd always thought he was a bit of an old fool, but he was really on my side over working and claiming at the same time. I know it went against his principles, but he could see I was in an impossible situation, caught in the poverty trap he called it. With my court case coming up, the solicitor again advised me to plead guilty, but I wasn't having it. So I decided to defend meself. Everyone said I was mad, particularly since I could go to prison if they find me guilty. But David stood by me and went off to the library to do some research about the law and that. He's a proper little Perry Mason on the quiet. And I was really proud of the way he stood up for me in front of the social workers. At times like this, you certainly find out who your friends are.

'I'm really making a big effort now. I'm off the booze and I'm doing me best for Louise. I don't care what anyone else thinks, I've turned over a new leaf. But deep down, I'm worried sick about the court case. What if they lock me up? What'll happen to Louise? It will have all been for nothing. I just hope to God it turns out all right.'

THE BROOKSIDE FILES

Patricia Farnham on Baby Alice

Patricia Farnham was overjoyed at the prospect of becoming a mum again, but the news that the baby would be Down's Syndrome stopped her in her tracks. After much deliberation, she decided to go ahead with the pregnancy, only to discover that husband Max was having difficulty accepting the new baby. Now living in France, Patricia recalls the traumas of raising little Alice.

'll never forget that afternoon in March 1994. Max and I were so looking forward to giving Thomas a brother or sister. After getting re-married, it seemed the perfect symbol of our renewed togetherness. When we went to the hospital, we thought it was just a routine serum test, nothing to worry about. But the doctor told us that the results of the test showed there was a slight risk of the foetus being abnormal. We were shaken rigid – it was the sort of news that every prospective parent dreads. First breast cancer and now this. What had I done to deserve such rotten luck?

'The doctor said he wanted me to have an amniocentesis and I agreed to go back the following day for the test. The

Mal Young: 'When we first talked at a storyline meeting about the idea of featuring a baby with Down's Syndrome, we got all kinds of response, from "let's not touch this" to "fantastic". When that happens, you know you'll get a similarly contentious response from the audience. One of the reasons we wanted to do it was to illustrate the recent advances in medical technology – that you can now have a test early in pregnancy to find out whether there are going to be problems with your baby. To carry a child that you know is going to be handicapped, knowing that you have the option to terminate the pregnancy, is a deeply emotive story and one which affected us all at the meeting. It was a scary one – none of the team had any personal experience of Down's Syndrome – and so we conducted a lot of research. Our researcher, Stephen Byrne, did a number of taped interviews with parents of children with Down's and in there was the inspiration for the path we took with Max. One woman said how her husband stayed out and shunned the child and we thought that was exactly how Max would react. We actually used two different children to play Alice and both sets of parents were able to give us further information. Of course when it was first revealed that the baby would be born with Down's Syndrome, everyone expected us to have Patricia fall downstairs and suffer a miscarriage. They thought that would be our way out, but we don't take the easy option on Brookside. Instead we wanted to show the positive aspects of the situation and the nice thing was that the Down's Syndrome Association wrote to us afterwards saying that the story had been a great help. And we must keep that going – we won't just forget about Alice. No matter what storylines we do with Max and Susannah, Max will still be the father of a child with Down's and that will affect his life for ever more.'

FAMILIES

Max never came to terms with Alice. It was ages before I could even persuade him to hold her.

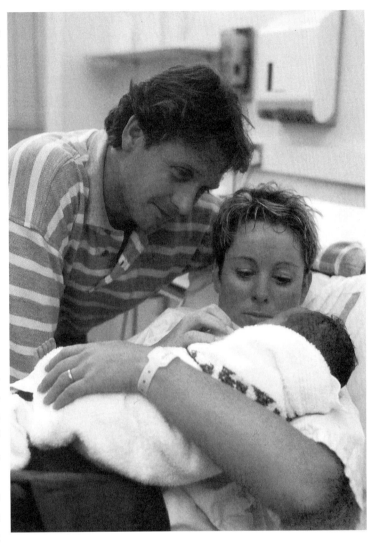

next couple of weeks were just about the longest of my life, praying that all would be well with the baby. Our ex-nanny, Margaret, was agonising over whether to go out to Bosnia to join her boyfriend Derek, so that took my mind off things for a bit...but not for long. To make matters worse, the night before I was due to get the results of this second test, our house was burgled – by our loveable local rogue, Jimmy Corkhill, as it turned out. So I was in a pretty miserable state of mind when I trooped back to the hospital. Then I got the results. The baby could have Down's Syndrome, and a couple of days later that probability became a certainty.

'Max was very supportive. He pointed out that I could have an abortion, but I didn't want one. It was my baby – our baby – and I couldn't bear to see it destroyed. I would still give it all the love in the world. We discussed the possible pitfalls, but when Max could see that I was eager to go ahead with the pregnancy, he went along with my decision. To convince him that everything would be alright, I took him along to see some children with Down's Syndrome at a school. The joy in their faces said everything. Even Max was moved.

'I didn't want to tell anyone apart from immediate family about the baby being Down's Syndrome. I must admit there were times during the pregnancy when I wondered whether I was doing the right thing for I was under no illusions as to the task ahead, the way the baby would change our lives forever. Whenever I looked at a 'normal' baby, like Bev's Josh, I couldn't help but feel envious. As the birth drew nearer, I got more and more scared.

THE BROOKSIDE FILES

'Alice was born in the August. I'd thought I would be strong, that I could cope, but all the planning and advice in the world can't prepare you for what lies ahead. At times like this, a woman needs a strong husband. I had Max. It wasn't long before his visits to the hospital became increasingly infrequent. He started inventing business trips to avoid coming to see us. I was really hurt and upset – I needed him there, to help me through it and so that he could get to know Alice. But he seemed to have washed his hands of us, doing his usual act of burying his head in the sand. I was so distraught that I locked myself in the hospital toilet and said that I wasn't coming out until they found Max. Eventually he turned up, all of a fluster. I demanded to know where he'd been and he said he needed time to adjust. Great!

'It did cross my mind that he wouldn't come and take us home. He certainly left it as late as possible and even when he did show up, he studiously avoided any physical contact with Alice. It was as if he thought he'd catch Down's

Syndrome from her. He clearly had no feelings for her, and even admitted as much.

'The first few weeks were hell. Every little cough, sneeze or tear and we rushed her back to hospital, only to be told there was nothing wrong.

With Max being away at every opportunity, Alice and I were left on our own.

FAMILIES

Alice just wouldn't stop crying. I wanted everyone to treat her normally and tried to integrate her into the family. I introduced Thomas to his new sister but all Max could offer in the way of support was the view that Thomas would have to look after Alice when we died. How could he be so insensitive!

'With the forthcoming opening of his own pet project, a new restaurant, Max had the perfect excuse for working all hours. He was out first thing in the morning and back late at night, nicely timing it so that he didn't have anything to do with Alice. I tried to pin him down, but he was just evasive. I know it was difficult for him – he hated the thought that the neighbours might pity him – but it was something we had to face together.

Alice's christening was one of the happiest days of my life – but I'm not sure how Max felt.

'Eventually, he said he wanted to be a proper father to Alice and to have her christened, but still he couldn't bring himself to hold her. We had a long, tearful chat and at last he picked her up. She must have been a month old by then. I felt that we were beginning to get somewhere.

'Whilst I was fully committed to being a mum, I couldn't help being jealous of Max's job. I missed work – having a baby was so restrictive. So I was delighted when Barry Grant – Max's partner – offered me the P.R. job for the restaurant. It stopped me feeling tied down. Nevertheless there were times when I felt guilty about not devoting 24 hours a day to Alice. But I needed to work for my own sanity. Also I thought that if I

Max's treatment of Alice was a contributory factor in the breakdown of the marriage.

was happy, I would be a better mother. Max resented my working, however – he thought my place was at home with the baby. On reflection, he had a point. I was definitely overdoing things and it all came to a head when I collapsed during

the christening. It was the only christening I know where the holy water had to be used to revive the mother!

'I was angry when Barry sacked me, saying it was for my own health, and bitter when I was turned down for work by another potential client, just because Alice started crying at the meeting. I was being penalised for trying to be a working mother. It was making me very unhappy, to the point where I started regretting ever going ahead with the pregnancy. It wasn't that I didn't love Alice, but she was even more time-consuming than I had imagined. There seemed no escape from her. She had taken over my life. I had lost my sense of independence – and that had always been very important to me. Suddenly, the future appeared to have very little to offer.

'I decided that putting Alice in a nursery would help her development and stimulate her, but the first one I tried rejected her. It was simple discrimination – they admitted Josh Dixon – and so unfair. Eventually I did manage to get her into a nursery, although I'm not sure that mum approved. At least it gave me time to get on with my life while I knew that Alice would be in capable hands, particularly as there were two other children with Down's Syndrome there.

'After nearly losing mum and Thomas to that dreadful virus that struck the neighbourhood, I took on a lot – the Gift Box and helping with the campaign to free Mandy and Beth. I realised how precious life was. The trouble was, although the nursery did a terrific job, Alice still needed a lot of attention from her parents. By the time I got home from work, I was exhausted and just wasn't able to devote sufficient time to Alice. When I took her to the hospital for one of her more important developmental check-ups – an appointment which Max, in typical fashion, managed to miss – the paediatrician told me in no uncertain terms that Alice had not been receiving enough stimulation. Somehow I felt we'd let her down.

'I really tried to make amends after that, spending as much time as possible with her. Max still wasn't interested though. Sure, he loved Alice but he wasn't willing to make any sacrifices. In truth, he was embarrassed by her – he somehow saw the fact that he was the father of a child with Down's as a failure on his behalf, a reflection on his manhood. Max Farnham, pillar of the community, successful restaurateur, but he didn't have a normal daughter. He couldn't handle it. He could be so weak and shallow. Even when he was supposed to do that bungee jump to raise money for Alice, he backed out at the last minute.

'I suppose all this simmering anger at the way he neglected Alice was partly to blame for the breakdown of our marriage. It wasn't just the business with the prostitute, even the constant calls on Susannah, it went deeper than that. He'd let me down once too often. What's more, he'd let Alice down too. Typically, when he tried to plead with me to stay, he suggested that Thomas and I should go for a holiday in the sun, to think things over. Not once did he mention Alice. Nothing had changed.

'She is still incredibly hard work, but I cherish the time I spend with her. It pains me to think that I once said I was sorry I had her, but we all say things we later regret. For the moment, she and Thomas mean everything to me. I just hope that one day Alice's father will be as proud of her as her mum is now.'

THE BROOKSIDE FILES

Susannah Farnham on Maintaining Good Relations With Your Ex

Susannah Farnham has always been there for Max – even when he didn't want her to be. As his former wife, she was able to twist him around her little finger, much to the irritation of his second wife, Patricia. When Patricia finally left for France, Susannah wasted no time in trying to take her place and rekindling the romance with Max. Here Susannah reveals the secret of maintaining good relations with your ex.

'Max and I go back a long way – further of course than Max and Patricia. However, I'm afraid that when Patricia acted the indignant wife whenever Max popped round to help me with one of my teensy problems, she conveniently forgot that he was mine before she stole him.

'Don't get me wrong, I like Patricia. I always have. She has great...spirit. It's just that I think I know what Max needs from a woman. He's such a sweetie, but he does need a shoulder to cry on, someone to reassure him, to tell him that everything's going to be alright. He's a bit like a child really, in the nicest possible way. The trouble with Patricia was that she was so busy with her own career that poor Max got neglected. And he really does need attention almost 24 hours a day. When he found that he couldn't talk to her, naturally he came round to see me and the children. I suppose I became his agony aunt, his Claire Rayner in a size 12.

'I know we slept together once while he was married to Patricia, but that really was the most dreadful mistake, if only because she found out. But it did prove what I already knew – that he still had feelings for me. However I wouldn't have dreamed of interfering or pushing myself forward in any way. When Patricia stormed off to France,

Mal Young: 'We knew that Gabrielle Glaister, who plays Patricia Farnham, wanted to take time off at the end of a long six years on the show. The Farnhams had a volatile relationship anyway, especially with Max's first wife, Susannah, always lurking in the background, so for Patricia to storm off and be replaced by Susannah seemed a natural development in Max's complicated love life. In the past, Susannah has always been a reactive rather than proactive character – reacting to what Max does and to what Patricia does – but this year, for the first time, the stories come from her. And I think we'll be surprised at how forthright and opinionated she is. When Patricia fears that her cancer has returned and that she may be dying, Susannah is horrifiedat the prospect of having to bring up Alice. She says she couldn't possibly do it. So that throws a new spanner into the relationship.'

FAMILIES

Max accused me of being devious and manipulative, and that hurt. I was genuinely sorry that they had split up.

'But you can't let a good man go to waste so, with myself and the children having nowhere to live, the obvious step was to move in with Max. It was like killing two birds with one stone. Max was rather lukewarm about the arrangement at first, complaining that he hadn't got any space to himself. Perhaps I did take things a little for granted, but I was appalled when he threatened to throw the children and me out. What sort of a father throws his own children on to the street? So in a fit of pique, Max moved out and into the

Patricia seemed to feel threatened by my presence. I can't think why.

flat above the pizza parlour. Only Max could throw himself out of his own house – he does get into a pickle sometimes.

'Unfortunately, David Crosbie didn't like the fact that I was in what he regarded as his daughter's house. So he moved out too. He was very unpleasant. I felt I had little option but to change the locks for my own safety. Of course, Max came grovelling back when he realised that he needed me to bail him out with the VAT man who had turned up at Grants to go through the books. I was happy to oblige, provided we got a few ground rules sorted out. Max was so grateful he cooked me a lovely meal that night. He really does look his best in an apron. And with David out of the way for once – he was at some geriatric gathering – Max and I were able to have a heart-to-heart. Fortified by the wine, I hinted at an emotional reconciliation and he didn't turn the suggestion down flat. I was beginning to make progress.

'But I felt I wanted to be more a part of Max's life. That was where Patricia went wrong – she almost seemed to resent the restaurant. So I asked him to let me become involved in the

FAMILIES

running of Grants. Besides, he needed organising – the paperwork was in a terrible mess. So I went to my solicitor and had the necessary documents drawn up to make me a full partner in the business. Max did his usual trick of blustering about it being totally unworkable before meekly giving in and signing. Getting my own way with Max has almost ceased to be a challenge. We celebrated with champagne and ended up in bed. It was just like the old times.

'Then I found out that a few days after our night of passion, Max had sex with Sammy Daniels. I couldn't believe it. Perhaps all those things Patricia said about him being untrustworthy were right after all. When he said he was sacking Sammy from her job as our cleaner, I asked him why. Of course, he was too much of a coward to tell me the truth and I could see him sweating, dreading that I would find out. In a perverse way, I was rather enjoying it, so I re-hired Sammy...just to see the look on Max's face. It was fun watching Max trying to wriggle out of yet another embarrassing situation, but I was determined to make him pay for his misdemeanours. I told him it was high time he took greater responsibility for Matthew and Emily and so I got him to cook their breakfast and iron their clothes. He didn't know what had hit him.

'Just like a man, Max thought that a spot of housework entitled him to jump into bed with me. Although I wasn't letting on that I knew about him and Sammy, there was no way I was allowing him back just when it suited him. I didn't want some casual part-time relationship. I'm afraid I really lost my temper and told him a few home truths. He always wanted to pick and choose – he had no idea about total commitment. I said it was the same when the children were babies. He avoided all the dirty jobs like looking after them when they were poorly and changing dirty nappies. All he wanted was the days out, the train set and the

Sammy Daniels tried to get her claws into Max, but it was no contest.

bedtime stories. It really was a blazing row and it ended with him saying he was going off to France to see Patricia. I was fed up with being messed around so I got all his new clothes, his books, his CDs and his expensive bottles of wine and gave them to Julia Brogan for the Over-55s auction. I thought, that'll teach him.

'He came back with his tail between his legs...until he looked in the wardrobe. While he went purple and waved his arms around, saying he hadn't got a thing to wear, I told him that I knew about his fling with Sammy. I said I was going to leave – I'd had enough of his philandering. Despite everything I felt for him, I was at the end of my tether. He realised that I was serious this time – this was not some clever ruse – and then he suddenly opened up and begged me not to go. He told me that it was me who had always blighted his marriage to Patricia. He wasn't being nasty about it, he just meant that while I was around, he could never give himself completely to her. We had too much history. For once I felt he was being honest. He really did want me to stay.

'I agreed that we would have to dispense with Sammy's services, but the poor girl didn't take it too well and started shouting from the rooftops that she was pregnant by Max. It turned out to be nothing more than a figment of her imagination and, strangely enough, the whole experience brought Max and me closer together. I think he was grateful that I'd stood by him through it all – something Patricia would never have done.

'We took the children for a week away at the Simpson family's cottage in the Cotswolds. It should have been like a second honeymoon, but we got the shock of our lives when we stumbled

I'm going to make sure I prove a better catch for Max than Patricia.

across Nat and Georgia Simpson in bed together. At least it shows the Farnhams aren't the only family on the Close with problems.

'I think we've put all of our difficulties of the summer behind us now and I can see us getting back together as a proper family. Patricia doesn't seem bothered about having him back, so there's nothing to stop us. And it will be better this time around, because when we married first time, we were too young and had no money. Now we know each other's little foibles – at least I know how to handle Max. Besides, he's already showing much more interest in the children which, the way things are going for Matthew at Brookside Comprehensive, is just as well. Yes, I think we've got a good future together and I hope that Max will soon achieve the unusual distinction of marrying two wives twice. One for the Guinness Book of Records perhaps?'

HEALTH

Jean Crosbie on the Mystery Virus

In the spring of 1995, a killer virus swept through Brookside Close. It turned out to be a legacy of Audrey Manners' husband George who had recently returned from Kenya. Among those struck down by the bug was Jean Crosbie. She eventually pulled through, but only after husband David had made a dramatic death-bed confession. For Jean, life would never be the same again. This is her story.

'To this day, I still can't believe it happened. With all the wonderful advances in medicine and technology, who would have thought that a virus from Africa could wreak such havoc among our community? The development of antibiotics has led us to believe that doctors can cure virtually anything, but apparently there are still millions of unknown virus strains throughout the world. And because there are so many, it is almost impossible to identify and therefore treat them in time. With modern-day travel, they can strike any time, anywhere. I was just lucky I pulled through.

'I remember the first person to be taken ill was young Carl

Mal Young: 'Some critics thought the idea of a mystery killer virus sweeping the Close was a bit far-fetched, but the fact is that modern transportation, allied to our penetration deep into the heart of rain forests, means that such a virus could travel from somewhere like Africa to our humble Close in no more than 24 hours. Phil came up with the idea early in 1994. We knew that by the spring of 1995, Trevor Jordache's body would have been dug up and with Mandy and Beth in jail, that story would relax a bit. We needed to remind people that there was more to Brookside than the Jordaches – we wanted to keep in the public eye. For maximum impact, we had to kill off popular characters like Audrey Manners and Garry Salter. And we deliberately cast Brian Murphy as George Manners because everybody remembers him from George and Mildred. And so viewers were sorry to see him die, too. As Phil Redmond pointed out at the time, it wasn't simply a case of sticking a pin in the cast list. We had to work out which type of people were most likely to fall victim to that type of virus – and that was the young and the elderly. We were able to look at how the various members of the community reacted to the crisis. Predictably, the Dixons ran while Mick Johnson became a hero. The viewing figures for the episodes were really high and, to prove our point, a couple of months later the newspapers were full of the mystery killer virus in Zaire.'

Banks. It was just after Rosie's 40th birthday party. Everyone had quite a bit to drink so we put it down to that. Then we heard that Garry Salter, a friend of Mick Johnson's, had suddenly collapsed and died at the leisure centre. The poor lad – he had only started work there that day. Still we had no reason to link it with Carl's illness.

'All the while George Manners was scurrying around the Close, trying to interest everyone in his wretched timeshare holidays in Kenya. Eddie Banks had decided to buy one but was horrified when he discovered that the video George had given him was completely blank. If only I'd known before George began his sales patter on me. He was so persistent, so plausible. Needless to say when he got back from some silly residents' association conference in Brighton, David said I should have seen right through the man. But he always did speak with the benefit of hindsight.

'Anyway George persuaded me that a holiday in Africa was exactly what I needed. I could just see David in his pith helmet and safari suit, every inch the old colonial, ordering the lions to remain seated while he took a photograph. George himself was looking decidedly peaky by now so I told him to rest at the bungalow while I popped in to town and drew out the £3,000. I knew there were risks attached – one hears about these timeshares – but it was exciting, a chance to do

George Manners had us all taken in with his sales patter, including Eddie Banks.

HEALTH

The deadly virus meant that the smiles didn't last long for George and Audrey Manners.

something adventurous for a change. David wouldn't have understood. When I got back from the building society, George was even worse. He looked like death and was doubled up in pain. No sooner had I handed him the money than he stumbled out of the front door into the arms of

Eddie Banks and Jimmy Corkhill. They denounced George as a fraud and snatched my money from him, saying he had conned them out of theirs. As Eddie let go, George slumped to the floor. He was dead.

'Audrey reckoned George probably died of terminal greed. She wasn't looking too good either and I insisted that she stay with us until she felt better. David was particularly peeved to find Audrey in our home. I couldn't understand what he'd suddenly got against the woman – they used to be such good friends. Indeed, I was the one who couldn't stand the sight of her at first. I

Although I'd grown quite fond of Audrey, little did I suspect that David was even closer to her.

thought she was nothing but an overbearing old busybody, but I'd since become quite fond of her. Between us, I liked the way we managed to keep David in check.

'David and Mick Johnson had got it into their heads that it was some deadly virus sweeping through the community. It was typical of David. He'd got nothing better to do so he decided to whip up a crisis, in the hope that all the residents would turn to him as their leader. Obviously he knows a thing or two about medicine from his years as a pharmacist, but he was diagnosing this outbreak as being anything from beri-beri to

HEALTH

Following David's pitiful confession, I decided to spread my wings and see the world.

hard-pad. I was sure that it was just flu. Patricia shared my views, even though Thomas wasn't too well either.

'Then I began feeling tired and a bit sweaty. David was fussing over me like a mother hen. I don't remember much after that. Apparently, I fainted and David found me lying unconscious on the kitchen floor.

'I soon came round and thought I was on the road to recovery. I kept telling David it was only flu. Everyone was getting hysterical. The health people sealed off the Close. Some people were pointing the finger at Mick's pizzas, others at Ron Dixon's shop. I really did think it was a lot of fuss about nothing. Then we heard that Thomas was

very ill and that Audrey had died. Perhaps it was more serious than I thought, but I didn't want to admit it and give David the satisfaction of being right.

'The next day, I came over very weak again. I gather I was drifting in and out of consciousness. David insisted that I go to hospital but I still had enough energy to refuse. If I was going to die, I wanted to die at home. Happily, he respected my wishes.

'One minute I felt hot and clammy and wanted to kick away all the bedclothes, the next I was bitterly cold. It certainly wasn't flu, more like some sort of fever. I kept feeling myself fall asleep. At times it must have been a deep sleep because I don't remember anything; at other times, it was much lighter because I was vaguely aware of what was going on around me. David was at my bedside. I could hear him prattling on. Waffle, waffle, waffle. Even in a state of semi-consciousness, I recall wishing that he'd get on with it and get to the point. You see, David can only talk when he has a meticulously-prepared script to read from. Ask him to ad-lib or be natural and he makes a mess of it. He certainly did on this occasion.

'It was obviously his farewell speech, but it suffered badly from lack of rehearsal. He began by going over the good old days, about how we'd met at a New Year's Eve party in Bristol. I kept expecting Michael Aspel to walk in with his big red book! He went on and told me how much he loved me, all fairly routine stuff, and then, displaying a rare touch of humility, apologised for not having been a better husband. He raked up that old business with Patricia's nanny but swore on the life of the national chairman of Residents' Associations that he had been utterly faithful ever since. But he seemed ill at ease, as if there was still something he wanted to get off his chest. Then I heard him mention Audrey Manners. He went round and round in circles, saying that it hadn't been important, that it had meant nothing to him, that she had virtually bound him to the bedpost and forced him. What was he going on about? It was supposed to be me who was deliriously ill, not him. Then I realised he was confessing to having slept with Audrey. Over and over again, he said he was sorry and then it all went quiet. I later discovered that, exhausted by the unburdening of his guilt, he had fallen asleep.

'The next morning, I felt Patricia come in and kiss me on the cheek. I think she was expecting me to be dead so it came as a bit of a shock to her when I suddenly opened my eyes and asked for a cup of tea. David came rushing in. He too was overjoyed, although behind the beaming smile, I detected the merest hint of a worried frown. How much of his death-bed confession had I heard?

'He was charm itself that morning. I got the five-star treatment. He kept gently skirting around the subject, testing the water with his toe but not daring to put his whole foot in. People imagine they hear the strangest things when they're at death's door, he said. They have weird dreams, hear odd voices. I felt like Joan of Arc! I wanted to string him along but I decided to put him out of his misery. Yes, I said, I had heard everything – the whole sad episode of his adultery with Audrey Manners.

'He wanted me to forgive him, but I refused. I remembered the fuss he'd kicked up about my old letters when he as good as accused me of being a rampant lesbian. I wasn't going to let him off lightly. I told him bluntly that he had only confessed about Audrey because he thought I was going to die – it was so that he could carry on living with a clear conscience. It was one of the most selfish acts I'd ever encountered. After my outburst, he shambled about the house looking like a lost labrador. Eventually he said he would do the honourable thing and move out. I was obviously expected to go down on bended knee, say that I couldn't possibly live without him, and implore him to stay. But I didn't. Instead I just let him go.

'There's nothing worse than a man wallowing in self-pity, and David presented a truly pathetic specimen. After a couple of days of watching him slouch around the Close like some poor old bag lady with nowhere to sleep, I relented and allowed him to come home. But it was on the condition that, from then on, we were totally honest with each other.

'Things were never quite the same again though. It wasn't that I had ceased to trust him, but being so near to death had made me realise how valuable life is. I wanted to savour every minute I had left, to spread my wings, see the world before it was too late. Although David could never appreciate it, there was life beyond the next meeting of the Brookside Residents' Association. So here I am, living life to the full in France, and not giving a damn about new council wheely bins, excessive noise after 10pm or dogs fouling the footpaths.'

HEALTH

Mick Johnson on the Dangers of Steroids

When he moved into number 5 with Sinbad, Mick Johnson started body-building in the garage. It began as a simple pastime, a method of keeping fit, but once he took to steroids and serious competition, it deteriorated into a dangerous obsession which threatened to destroy his family.

'Ever since I won a heat one year at Butlin's way back, I'd always fancied having a go at body-building. I liked to keep in good nick – it gave me a buzz. I didn't take it that seriously at first – as much as anything it was a way of getting Sinbad to stop looking eight-months pregnant – but when Val Walker, Jackie Corkhill's sister, said she worked out at a proper gym, I decided to give it a go. The equipment there was really awesome. I couldn't believe some of the weights that were being lifted and I felt out of my depth. This was a different world. Val said I should put my name down for a novices' competition – it would give me something to work towards. She warned me to take it easy at first but, like a fool, I wouldn't listen. I ended up over-

doing it and pulled a muscle in me shoulder.

'I should have taken a month off, but I knew if I did that, I'd miss the competition. And I'd really set me heart on doing well in it. It gave me a goal in life and helped me forget about our Leo who'd been skiving off school, encouraged by that Danny Simpson and his fancy middle-class ideas about teaching yourself. Val said there were some people at the gym who reckoned there was only one short-cut to overcoming an injury in a hurry...steroids.

'I wasn't sure. I mean, you hear so many horror stories about people who've taken steroids. But at the same time, I was well into the training and I hated the idea of missing the competition. They were easier to get hold of than I thought – £70

Mal Young: 'We thought Mick Johnson was the sort of guy who would try something new in life. We looked at Louis Emerick, who plays Mick, and realised how fit he was. So we decided to put a flip side on the drugs issue. Across the Close there was Jimmy Corkhill and the more common face of drugs; here was our chance to look at a different type of drug addiction – steroid abuse. We also wanted to show how Mick copes as a single parent. The fact is he's over-protective towards Leo and Gemma. He tries to over-compensate for his ex-wife Josie not being there. As a result, his expectations of them and indeed himself are far too high. But because he's basically a nice guy, to see him lash out at his kids has a bigger impact than if, say, Jimmy did. You just don't expect it from Mick. Louis often asks me whether there's going to be a storyline where Mick can smile but I remind him that the best stories are the dramatic ones.'

for a six-week course. I was still a bit wary, but Terry Sullivan told me he knew a doorman who took steroids and was perfectly healthy. Anyway, I thought it wasn't as if I was going to get hooked on them.

'I really pushed meself in training, but it was so frustrating when the injury prevented me lifting heavier weights. I thought the answer was to take more steroids. I know some people reckon taking steroids is cheating, but I didn't see it like that. I mean, I bet all the other competitors were doing the same. Val was a good sounding-board. She said that I had to be careful about getting dependent on steroids, but I was planning to jack them in once the competition was over. They were only to help me get over the injury. She also warned me that one of the side effects is that they can make you aggressive. I laughed it off. Me, aggressive? Everyone knows I'm the gentle giant.

'With the date of the competition just a week away, everything seemed to be piling up on top of me. I was so desperate for staff at the pizza parlour that I took on Jimmy Corkhill. And that was only 'cos Hannibal Lecter wasn't available. Then Leo turned up at the shop with that Danny Simpson. Leo had been in a fight and I reckoned it was all Danny's fault. Ever since he'd arrived on the Close, there'd been nothing but trouble. Danny started giving me some lip and I lost me rag and clipped him round the ear. I know I shouldn't have done it, but he was asking for it, the cheeky little beggar. Next thing I've got Danny's dad, Ollie, on me doorstep, accusing me of being a thug and a bully. I wasn't taking that from no-one and I pinned him against the wall. I asked him whether he wanted to sort it out man-to-man, but he just threatened me with solicitors.

I might have known he hadn't got the stomach for a fight.

'I was getting fed up with people starting lecturing me about things. Even Sinbad had a pop, saying I was a cheat for using steroids and that I should flush them down the loo. What did he know?

HEALTH

'I felt really up for the competition. I definitely thought I could win it. Just before it started, I decided to do a few last-minute lifts, to get me psyched up, like, but as I was pumping up, I suddenly felt this excruciating pain in me shoulder. It was the old injury flared up again. I'd have to miss the competition. I was gutted.

There was a lot of bullying going on at school, mainly involving that Tinhead kid.

'I knew the only thing to do was to stay on the steroids to build me up and get straight back into the gym. Nothing was going to stop me next time. I got Leo into it too. I thought if he did some

Weight training gave me a new purpose in life but steroids almost destroyed me.

weight training, nobody at school would be able to beat him up. He wasn't keen, but he went along with it. Looking back, I think he was probably scared of saying no to me. I must have been horrible to live with. Leo and Gemma were frightened to say or do anything in case I suddenly flew off the handle. Leo caught me popping steroids one day and asked me what they were for. I said they were just like vitamin pills. I was even having to lie to me own kids – that was what steroids were doing to me.

'Things came to a head when I found out that Leo had been involved with the burglary at the Simpsons' house. I knew it was the fault of a kid at Leo's school they call Tinhead. I don't know what his real name is. Fortunately I managed to persuade Bel not to call the police. But I was still

furious with Leo for allowing Tinhead to bully him into taking part. I told him he was a wimp and a coward – no son of mine. It was a dreadful thing to say, but I was so angry.

'We had a row about steroids. I told Leo I took them to toughen meself up like a man. I said he should try it. I didn't mean he should try steroids. I just wanted him to be able to defend himself. While I was out, he must have found my supply 'cos he took a couple and started lifting weights far too heavy for him in the garage. Next thing he's in hospital with a broken collar bone and concussion.

'It was when I saw him in that state that it dawned on me what an idiot I'd been. He was sobbing his heart out, saying he'd let me down, but in truth it was me who had let him down. And what would have happened if Gemma had got hold of me steroids – after all I'd just left them lying about the house? It didn't bear thinking

HEALTH

Things got so bad that Leo and Gemma preferred to be with Sinbad than me.

about. That was it as far as I was concerned – no more steroids. The first chance I got, I was going to flush them down the loo.

'I was all set to pull out of the competition, but Val convinced me to carry on – to show the kids I could do it without steroids. It seemed to make sense, but, most of all, it was what I wanted to hear. But I still hadn't been able to bring meself to flush the steroids away. In the end, I came third and was well pleased with meself. Leo and Gemma weren't so impressed. I hadn't had time to take them anywhere in the school holidays, but I promised to make it up to them by taking them to a theme park. Then I heard from the gym that the guy who came second in the novices' competition had dropped out of the area finals, and would I like to take his place? I was made up...then I realised that it was the same day that I was supposed to be going out with Leo and Gemma. I hadn't the heart to tell them.

'Then a couple of days before the finals, I found the excuse I'd been waiting for. Gemma spilt hot fat over the kitchen floor. It was an accident, and I felt really bad about it, but the kids thought I was just having another go at them. So I didn't disappoint them. I said that to punish them, the trip to the theme park was off. I was going to the area finals instead.

'Sinbad stepped in as surrogate father – I think they preferred being with him than me – and said I could still go along if I wanted. But I was too involved with me weights. He told me that body-building meant more to me than me own children. In me heart, I knew he was right. Worse still, I'd started back on steroids. I just couldn't face the fact that I was dependent on them.

'There was another big row when they got back that evening. Sinbad said Leo and Gemma wanted to stay the night with him and Fee. I thought Sinbad had been filling their heads with stories about me. I wanted my kids in my home. I had a right go at Sin. In fact we might have come to blows if Leo hadn't knocked me out with me third-place trophy. I was that embarrassed at me own son hitting me that I made up some story about falling over at home. Soon word had got around that I'd fought off another burglar – just like a few years back. If only they'd known the sad truth. Mick Johnson, Mr. Nice Guy, but his kids wanted nothing to do with him.

'The thump on the head finally brought me to me senses. I agreed to let Leo and Gemma stay at Fee's for a few days as a sort of cooling-off period. I missed them like mad. I knew I had to show them that things would be different so I sold all me gym equipment and packed in the steroids. Leo came round and we had a good talk. He said he was sorry for hitting me, but I reckoned I probably deserved it. He was blaming himself and Gemma for the fact that Josie and Marianne had walked out on me, but I told him that was rubbish. I'd been a lousy father to him over the last few months, always losing me temper for no reason, thinking about nothing other than that competition. God knows, the poor kid had been through enough in the past without me putting him through all that.

'Things haven't been easy for me – not really since Josie left. More than ever, I need my friends and my family. From now on, I'm determined to make it up to Leo and Gemma. They're great kids – and I want to show them that they're the most important thing in the world to me. And I never want to see another steroid as long as I live.'

HEALTH

Katie Rogers on Bulimia

Katie Rogers has never had much to smile about. Following the break-up of her parents' marriage and the death of her father, she was betrayed by the one man she trusted, cult leader Simon Howe. Her health and happiness suffered again when she became bulimic. Here she re-lives her experiences of the eating disorder.

'When Simon died, I thought I was finally rid of him. I didn't feel anything. I wasn't happy, I wasn't sad. There was just a numbness. And to think that once me, and the rest of his gullible disciples, would have done absolutely anything for him. In my case, that meant sleeping with him. He told me it was God's will. At the time I was so vulnerable that I

thought: who am I to argue with God?

'Things were really going well for me last year. I'd got a job as a dancer in a Christmas panto and I'd got a new boyfriend, Christian, who was one of the cast. We had a weekend away at the beginning of December. After the way Simon had treated me, I was wary about letting any boy get too close to me. But it was

Mal Young: 'The art of our job is to look inside a character and ask: "What is going to happen to this person?" We spoke about Katie Rogers for a long time, recognising that this girl was the product of a dysfunctional family. Her father had been killed tragically, her brother Geoff, a failed footballer, had gone off the rails, sister Sammy was married with a child (a situation she was forced into) and had moved away, and her mum had gone off to Japan. And here was Katie, totally unsupported and going through her formative years. And we thought, there are going to be problems here. Katie is a dancer and that profession is all about image, so we started to look at image. We chatted about eating disorders and began to look at facts and figures. Stephen Byrne, our researcher, brought us lots of information on the subject from all angles, including interviews with parents and the medical profession. We learned about the telltale signs of bulimia. As you're sick a lot, you get cold sores around the mouth and because you're putting your fingers down your throat, you have chafing on your knuckles where they catch on your teeth. And you get bags under the eyes. So our make-up and wardrobe departments came into their own to make Diane Burke, who plays Katie, look bulimic. Apparently, people with eating disorders start to dress up a lot and wear more make-up to cover the spots they get from vitamin deficiency. And they carry around mouth-freshener mints to cover up the fact that they are being sick. It was a difficult story to portray on screen because it is so secretive. Also, once you've seen Katie be sick a few times, it's very unpleasant to watch, so we didn't think we could sustain it for too long. People can go on undetected for seven years or more but we decided to have Katie found out pretty quickly. It was very rewarding, however, because we received letters of praise from parents and organisations alike, thanking us for showing the telltale signs. Again, a successful helpline was run at the end of specific episodes.'

different with Christian. I really liked him and I could tell he liked me. So somehow sleeping together felt right. And it was every bit as good as I'd hoped, except that the condom slipped off and I had to take the morning-after pill. When I got back to the Close, I couldn't wait to tell Jacqui what a great time I'd had, but her face was nearly touching the floor. She said Terry Sullivan had been round to tell her that a girl Simon knew had died of AIDS. And the girl had caught it from Simon. That meant I could be infected too.

'My heart sank. I was convinced I was going to die. Terry said I should go for a test but I thought, what's the point? There's no cure. I was angry and afraid at the same time. Simon hadn't just destroyed my life and that girl's, he'd probably killed Christian too.

'Christian kept calling round to see me. He couldn't understand what was wrong, and I couldn't tell him. I ended up telling him to go away – I just wanted to be left alone. I tried finishing with him, but he wouldn't stop pestering me, demanding to know why I was breaking it off. One night, I took a deep breath and told him the truth – that I might have AIDS. He was shattered and hurt and called me selfish for not telling him. He went off and had a blood test and it was negative, but I still couldn't face it. Finally, Terry persuaded me to go. I was so relieved when it was negative that I rushed round to tell Christian the good news, hoping that we could get back together again. But he wanted nothing more to do with me – he said what I did to him was attempted murder. I was devastated. I thought we were good friends. I thought he really cared. How could he say that about me?

'I'd been right off me food with the worry, and now I found I didn't want much. Added to which, this dancing role was dead important to me, and I had to watch me weight. There's no jobs for fat dancers. So when people told me I was looking a bit thin, I said I was on a strict diet for the show. But it got so bad I collapsed on the opening night. I just didn't have the strength to dance and under the hot lights I came over all faint. After that it seemed that everyone decided I needed fattening up. They kept plying me with food – pizzas, burgers, the lot – but I managed to avoid eating any of that stuff. I said I'd have something later. But then I started to have these mad binges, raiding everything in the kitchen that had

Terry tried to persuade me to go for an AIDS test, but at first I was too frightened.

food...even the bin. In a way, the food made me feel contented, even happy.

'Just after Christmas, me, Jacqui and Rachel had a carpet picnic. Again they kept encouraging me to eat, but I made the excuse that I'd had plenty while preparing it all. I was lying through me teeth, but I couldn't help meself. When we'd finished and they went clubbing, I binged on all the left-over food...and then, when the guilt about what I'd done hit me, rushed to the bathroom to stick me fingers down me throat. Chocolate bars were me favourite. I'd eat half a dozen and then sick them all up in the toilet. Other times, I polished off three pizzas in one go and a whole

I'd wanted to lose weight for the panto but I was so weak I could hardly stand up.

I couldn't stop bingeing on left-over food. Then I'd rush to the toilet and stick me fingers down me throat.

pack of chocolate eclairs, still frozen. I was spending half me life in that bathroom.

'I kept looking at meself in the full-length mirror. I didn't like what I saw. FAT, FAT, FAT. How could I ever be a dancer with a body like a beached whale? I just sat alone in my bedroom for hours on end and cried. I was so lonely. Dad was dead, Mum had made a new life for herself, and I never heard from our Sammy. My so-called mates, Jacqui and Rachel, were out clubbing all hours, and I'd got nothing, nobody. Whoever would fancy me looking the way I do? Fellas only like slim girls. Then, to rub it in, Jacqui pulls the star of the show, Shane Cochran. She always did get the best blokes. I thought a visit to me mum might cheer me up, but all I got was bad news. She told me she was moving to Japan of all places – another person I love moving out of my life.

'Jacqui and Rachel were getting increasingly worried about me, they'd heard me being sick a

couple of times. Jacqui asked me if I was pregnant, but I bit her head off and told her to find something else to gossip about. I didn't want people fussing over me, least of all Lee Banks. He kept following me everywhere, spying on me – it was dead creepy. I know he meant well, but I thought he was just a silly kid.

'As it turned out, I owe him a lot. He was the only one who'd seen my hidden hoards of food, but I made him promise not to tell anyone. I said it was our secret. And cos he fancied me, he went along with it. But then I fainted again, this time at the end of the pancake race on the Close. It was then that Lee told people I had an eating disorder. Ron Dixon was really good to me – he was like a second father to me. Even though he had all that

dreadful business with his Mike being locked up in Bangkok, he still took me under his wing and let me stay at his place. At least I didn't feel quite so alone. He took me to see a clinical psychologist at a specialist eating disorders clinic, but when they asked me to fill in a form, I panicked and ran out. I just didn't want to share my problems with a complete stranger. I did all I could to get out of going again – I pretended everything was fine – but Bev caught me hiding more food and got me to see sense. She told me she'd help me through it. A lot of people on the Close don't like Bev, but she's good-hearted really.

Everyone rushed to help me when I fainted at the end of the pancake race.

HEALTH

I had a crush on my counsellor, Mark Smith. I felt silly, but he was dead good about it.

'Next time, she went along to the clinic with me. I know Mr. Dixon was kind and all that, but I felt more at ease with a woman being there. But the nicest surprise was my counsellor, Doctor Mark Smith. He was young, good-looking and dead ordinary. I couldn't believe he was a doctor. There was none of this "Dr. Smith" – it was always "Mark".

'I felt really comfortable with him. I could talk to him. He told me his sister had an eating disorder. I liked finding out personal things about him – it made me feel close to him. I really began to look forward to our little meetings. The bottom line was I fancied him. By now I'd moved back into the bungalow, because I really felt I was on the mend, and we were having a party. It seemed like the perfect opportunity to ask Mark. He politely declined, saying he'd got an important meeting, but I saw him picked up by a girl in a car. I was so upset. It was yet another person who didn't want

to know me. At the party, I locked meself in me room and went on another binge. I was past caring. I wouldn't let anyone in – I just wanted to be left alone. Eventually Mark came round. He was so good with words, his voice was so calming that I found myself talking to him. He wanted to know why I'd stopped going to the sessions. I admitted it was because I had a crush on him. He told me it was more than his job was worth to get involved with a patient, and I knew he was right. He hadn't rejected me at all. I'd just been silly. He said he'd devise a meal plan for me and in return I agreed to keep a record of all the food I was eating. I promised him I'd try really hard.

'I still go to counselling, but I know the worst is behind me now. Mark tells me I'm a model client, and that makes me feel dead good. It's such a relief to be in control of my eating. And my dancing career's looking up. All I've got to do now is sort out our Sammy...'

MONEY

David Crosbie on the National Lottery

David Crosbie was convinced that winning the lottery was simply a matter of applying logical principles of mathematics. His faith was swiftly rewarded when the syndicate which the Crosbies had formed with Rosie and Eddie Banks yielded a £100,000 win. The only principle David had overlooked was that of human greed...

'Even now it pains me to recount that shameful chain of events whereby Jean and I were so nearly swindled out of what was rightfully ours. It was an episode which, frankly, brought no credit whatsoever upon the Banks household and, given the subsequent loss of their home through financial difficulties, could ultimately be said to have resulted in a certain degree of poetic justice.

'I wish to emphasise from the outset that I am not by nature a gambling man. To my mind, the football pools have always catered for the baser elements of society, compiled, as they invariably are, in smoke-filled alehouses and requiring a minimum of skill and knowledge. The very fact that the entrant is obliged to mark their entry with a cross suggests in itself an inability to master the simpler tasks of the English language. However I have always found the National Lottery an altogether more appealing proposition, and not merely because the erstwhile presenter, that Turner woman, has a rather shapely pair of legs and, I might add, a winning smile. Thus when Jean and Rosie Banks decided that the two

Mal Young: 'There is no doubt that the National Lottery has had a big effect on people's lives, and in some cases it has brought out the worst side of human nature. We've read in the newspapers about instances where couples or syndicates have refused to share their winnings with their partners and been taken to court. As a contemporary drama reflecting the issues of today, we wanted to incorporate the lottery and at the same time we wanted to show both sides to it – how winning a lot of money can be a mixed blessing. We chose two socially opposite families like the Banks and the Crosbies because we knew there was more scope for potential conflict. And the audience was able to put themselves in the position of Eddie and Rosie. Would you share £100,000 if you didn't have to? It's a great moral dilemma.'

MONEY

families should form a lottery syndicate, I was wholeheartedly in favour of the idea.

'Where most people go wrong with the lottery is that they fail to exercise their imagination, sadly an all-too-familiar national trait these days. When choosing numbers, they opt for birthdays and anniversaries, thereby greatly reducing the chances of success. My view, and one shared by the Banks boy who turned out, somewhat against the odds I might say, to be a computer buff, was that all 49 numbers needed to be utilised in order to maximise the possibilities of hitting the jackpot.

'Naturally, my judgement proved spot-on. By a systematic selection of numbers, our little syndicate won £10 at the first attempt. It was surely the little acorn from which our mighty monetary oak would grow.

'The second week was a disappointment, but it did not diminish my enthusiasm for the project one iota, and I remained supremely confident that success lay just around the corner. That weekend, Jean and I were in Bath on a trip arranged by the Golden Oldies, but before departing I left young Rachel Jordache with a clear, written inventory of duties to be undertaken. They included handing, in person, the required £2 lottery stake money to Eddie Banks. Satisfied that there was no room for misconception, I felt able to depart to Bath.

'Watching the television that Saturday evening, I could hardly believe my eyes. Five winning numbers and the bonus ball. Of course, it was by no means entirely unexpected – not with the system to which I had ensured we adhere – but even I must confess to having been a mite surprised at the speed of it all. We were full of plans for the future. Jean, needless to say, was talking excitedly about trips to foreign climes, whereas I preferred to keep my feet a little firmer on the ground. For example, a new pair of oven gloves was an absolute necessity.

'When we arrived back at the Close, I was expecting tickertape and bunting at the very least, provided, of course, that

Young Lee Banks went up in my estimation with his knowledge of computers.

adequate provisions were made to clear up the litter after the celebrations. Instead the place was strangely quiet. With hindsight, the silence was ominous. Rachel eventually arrived back an hour or so later and appeared distinctly apathetic regarding our good fortune. Then we saw the Banks pull up in a four-wheel drive monstrosity, more suited to big-game hunting in the Serengeti than negotiating rush-hour traffic in Liverpool. Eddie was full of himself, proclaiming their lottery win. When I corrected him that it was our lottery win too, he coolly mentioned that Rachel had forgotten to hand over the stake money and that, assuming the syndicate to be cancelled, they had therefore put in the extra themselves. He

It was thoroughly distasteful the way the Banks paraded their new found wealth, especially as half the money was ours!

thus insisted that the £100,000 was all theirs. The cheek of the man!

'We tried reasoning with them, pointing out that we had a binding, verbal contract, but to no avail. Jimmy Corkhill suggested that a more productive method of persuasion might be via the use of a baseball bat, but, despite my disgust at their behaviour, I was not prepared to sink to their level. However if necessary I was prepared to bring the weight of the law of the land bearing down on the shoulders of Eddie and Rosie Banks.'

MONEY

'Jean endeavoured to re-open the channels of negotiation by inviting the Banks to dinner, in the hope that we could somehow come to an amicable solution. Fat chance! Eddie dug in his heels like a donkey on Southport beach. To add insult to injury, he revealed that he had won using my numbers!

'It was a thoroughly miserable week but as the weekend approached, I rather cleverly managed to put Eddie on the spot by handing over our next batch of £2 stake money. It was clearly the last thing he was expecting. He was so flustered that he refused to accept it. I therefore demanded that he choose different numbers, whereupon he slammed the door in my face. Nevertheless, I had made my point.

'Indeed it seemed that I had touched an unexpected nerve of sensitivity for, two hours later, Rosie and Eddie appeared on our doorstep with a cash offering. It was five big ones all right – but minus a couple of noughts. If they thought we would accept a miserly £500, they had woefully underestimated the calibre of person with whom they were dealing. To illustrate my contempt for the offer, I hurled the notes into the air, the breeze scattering them across the Close. As I shut the door, all I could see were these two pitiful figures, crawling along the gutter in an undignified attempt to rescue their ill-gotten gains. I saw it as rather symbolic.

'However we were by no means alone in our contempt for the Banks. They threw a party, presumably in an obscene effort to court public favour, to which no one turned up. Like a good general, I opted to capitalise on my opponents' discomfort by ramming home my psychological advantage. I reiterated my threat of legal action, claiming that my solicitor had told me we had an

I'm afraid Eddie and Rosie's refusal to honour our contract led to a few harsh words.

THE BROOKSIDE FILES

excellent case. It was of course a complete bluff but, although I say so myself, I was rather convincing.

'Yet success was not immediate. Our foes appeared as intransigent as ever and I was beginning to tire of the whole unseemly episode. If they wanted the money that badly, they could have it. I refused to let the good name of the Crosbies be dragged into the mire along with that of our ne'er-do-well neighbours. I could at least claim a moral victory. I was on my way over to the

Banks to inform them that I would no longer be pursuing our claim when I met Rosie half-way. Before I could say a word, she insisted on handing me the full £50,000, saying that they'd had a change of heart. It is nice to know such a thing exists in that household.

'As Jean and I toasted our triumph and she laid out plans for months of foreign travel, neither the Banks nor myself could have envisaged what a mixed blessing that lottery win would prove. Thanks to it, I no longer have a wife and they no longer have a house. I have to conclude that whoever said money isn't everything is a wiser man than I.'

When I hurled their £500 into the air, the Banks began scrambling for the notes in the gutter.

MONEY

Rosie Banks on Her Gambling Addiction

Most people would have been satisfied with a £50,000 lottery win but Rosie Banks wanted more. Driven by the misguided conviction that she couldn't lose, she proceeded to gamble away her windfall, her husband and her home, in the process alienating all around her. Here she describes the worst six months of her life.

'When I go to meetings of Gamblers Anonymous, as part of my rehabilitation I talk about my experiences and how I became a compulsive gambler in the first place. I'd always enjoyed the odd flutter on things like the Derby and the Grand National, but it was scratchcards that first got me hooked. When I won £50 one time, I thought it was easy. So I kept on buying them and I kept on winning. Then, of course, our lottery numbers came up. That made me sure I was on a winning streak. I could feel it in me bones.

'It was very nice winning 50 grand, but I thought I could make it into 100. At the time everything I touched seemed to be turning to gold. I started going to the bingo with our Mo on a regular basis – three, four, even five nights a week. I even sneaked into any arcades I was passing while on me traffic warden beat so that I could play the fruit machines. And still I kept winning. The trouble was, I wasn't keeping track of how much I was spending.

'I bought stacks of Chrissy pressies at the end of October, just because it felt so great to have plenty of money for the first time in me life. Eddie wasn't keen on me going out to bingo all hours, so I started making up stories, telling lies. Although I didn't know it, I was already on the slippery slope to financial ruin. And what I

Mal Young: 'We knew that Susan Twist and Paul Broughton, who played Rosie and Eddie Banks, wanted to move on, to leave Brookside. At the same time, we were thinking to ourselves: "Have we done everything with the Banks that we set out to?" We decided that we had, but we wanted to take them out with a bang. So Rosie's gambling fitted in nicely with their lottery win. Research underlined how devious compulsive gamblers can become – how they'll often go to extraordinary lengths to cover their tracks. And so we had Rosie turning into this really unpleasant, cunning woman who, at one point, was even prepared to let her own son take the rap for her thieving. When she went to the casino for the last time, I think a lot of the audience expected her to win the money back in a Hollywood-style happy ending. But that's not the way we do things on Brookside – we like to come up with the unexpected. So when they did lose the house and were forced to move out, it came as a shock to a lot of viewers. We were merely reflecting reality. Life isn't always full of happy endings.'

THE BROOKSIDE FILES

I began spending most of me life – and money – at the bingo. And if I didn't win, I was sure that big jackpot was just around the corner. What a fool I was!

also didn't realise was that my gambling obsession was driving Eddie into the arms of my daughter-in-law. But that's another story.

'Sometimes I'd lose at bingo. Maybe I'd be one number short of a full house, but I was sure it was only a matter of time before I hit the jackpot. It got to the stage where I couldn't bear missing a night in case someone else won the prize which I saw as being rightfully mine. I suppose in view of the amount of stake money I'd contributed to the kitty over the weeks, I almost did have a valid claim! Then I did win. Mo

MONEY

said I was a jammy so-and-so but I knew I was a natural winner.

'Relations with Eddie were becoming strained, particularly after he discovered I'd taken our granddaughter Becca into an arcade. I tried to lie me way out of it, but he didn't fall for it. He told me I'd got a problem. I said the only problem I'd got was him. If I wasn't gambling, I was getting withdrawal symptoms. I couldn't make a simple journey round to the pizza parlour without buying a bundle of scratchcards or having a go on the quiz machine. But I didn't see it as a problem. As far as I was concerned, it was just a harmless bit of fun.

'All the time, I had to find the legal aid contribution each month. I was suing the hospital for damages after they performed an unauthorised hysterectomy on me, and I was determined not to give up without a fight. It's not in my nature to surrender quietly. Our winnings were slipping through my fingers faster than you can say 'two little ducks' and so Eddie persuaded me to deposit the money in Mo's account where I couldn't get at it. I wasn't happy about it at all. And it didn't end there. Next thing, he's confiscated me cash card and is telling me he doesn't trust me. I wasn't having that. Besides, I couldn't get by without me daily fix. I talked Mo into withdrawing some cash from the account, pretending that Eddie had said it was OK. Being me sister, she believed me. It's awful when gambling makes you deliberately deceive your own family.

'Things were beginning to get desperate. I was having a bad run at the bingo and knew I had to win it back before Eddie realised I'd blown

---

If it wasn't the bingo, it was fruit machines. Still I was convinced that I didn't have a problem.

another big hole in our winnings. Night after night I lost. I knew I couldn't keep losing forever. My luck would change soon. But I'd almost run out of time. Less than two months after our £50,000 win, there was just £27 left in our account. I knew Eddie would kill me if he found out.

'I had to get that money back somehow so I took a second job, at Grants. But I blew part of me first week's wages on a dozen useless scratchcards. How could I have been such a mug!

'I thought the tide was turning when I won £1,000 at bingo. I was sure I was back on me winning streak. Mo was dead narky with me though and refused to lend me any money for Christmas bingo. I had to be there because I

knew I would win, so I raised the cash by stealing a few portions of steak from the restaurant. I didn't think Max Farnham would miss them.

'Max had put me in a position of responsibility so stealing from the store room was easy. And it paid for bingo. I called it me steak money. Unfortunately penny-pinching Max was soon on the warpath. I hadn't realised how low I'd sunk till I almost let our Lee carry the can for my pilfering. Max had caught him in the stock room and had jumped to the conclusion that he was the thief. I kept hoping it would blow over, but when Max said he was going to the police, I finally had to own up. I was so ashamed of meself. I couldn't look either Eddie or Lee in the eye. I was an outcast in me own home. That was the final nail in the coffin for Eddie and me. We'd already had to cancel our dream holiday after I was forced to admit I'd spent all our money. He said everything

I'd bought had to go back – even our Lee's computer. I was so humiliated.

'I became aware of the whispering about me on the Close. Suddenly everyone seemed to know about our money problems. I blamed Eddie for telling people. We had a blazing row and he moved out to stay with Sarah, our daughter-in-law. He said he'd only come back if I were to get help with my gambling addiction, but I refused point blank. I still didn't see I had a problem.

'Our Lee had disowned me too. He was threatening to leave unless I managed to get back together with Eddie. It was bad enough losing my husband, but I couldn't bear losing my son too, so I made a real effort to win Eddie back. But he was cold towards me, distant. Then I found out why – he told me he was in love with another woman.

'Soon after that, he did come back though things were pretty strained. We slept apart, but then again we hadn't had sex for months anyway, not since my hysterectomy. I kept my side of the bargain by going to Gamblers Anonymous, but then it all blew up again when I found that the 'other woman' was Sarah. I stormed off and went to stay with Mo.

'It was Lee who got us back together temporarily – he's a good lad. And whatever had gone on between Eddie and me, neither of us wanted to hurt Lee. He'd had enough troubles of his own in the past. Now what he needed was a stable home life. Unfortunately he was living in the wrong house for that. The relative peace was shattered when a bailiff's letter arrived. It was a

Eddie and me used to be so happy – till my gambling wrecked it all.

MONEY

repossession order to quit the house in 14 days. Over the past six months, I'd been gambling away the mortgage money and ignoring all the registered letters from the building society. We were £3,000 in arrears.

'The only way out seemed to be via the hospital who had upped their offer of compensation to £25,000. I thought what they'd done to my body was worth more, but the solicitor advised me to accept. I still wasn't happy. I knew if we could have held out for £50,000, we could have bought the house outright.

'That's when I made the worst mistake of my life. Sinbad had been to a new casino with Terry and told me how he could have won £500 but bottled out. That whetted my appetite. If a novice like Sinbad could win, think what I could do. I decided to bet the 25 grand on the roulette wheel, determined to double our money on one turn of the wheel. I lost the money...and with it went our house. Back home, Eddie went berserk, smashing up the place and, in the heat of the row, Lee found out about Eddie and Sarah. What a mess!

'We sold off everything. I couldn't stand watching the likes of Julia Brogan going through our things like vultures. This wasn't some tatty bring and buy sale, they were our possessions. And I knew it was all my fault. We left the Close quietly – we didn't want anyone to see us go. We were ashamed to be seen by people whom we had recently counted as friends. Despite

I saw one last chance to save our house on the spin of a roulette wheel.

my stupidity and lies which had cost us the house, Eddie gave me a cheque to help me on my way. To do so, he had sold his beloved Harley. I was really touched. I suddenly realised how much I still loved him and I could see he felt the same. After what we'd been through, we could handle anything the future threw at us.

'I've been given a second chance. I'm not sure I deserve it, but I've come to realise that gambling can take over your life, to the point where it becomes an illness. From now on, it's nothing more than 10p each-way on the Boat Race.'

THE BROOKSIDE FILES

NEIGHBOURS

Jackie Corkhill on Freeing the Jordaches

In the summer of 1995, Patricia Farnham, Jean Crosbie and Jackie Corkhill spearheaded the campaign to free Mandy and Beth Jordache. Patricia, in particular, had grave reservations about Jackie's involvement. After all, the Corkhills were unlikely to go down in history for their contribution to public speaking. Yet in the event, it was Jackie's voice which emerged the loudest, her sheer passion for the cause having a greater impact even than Patricia's carefully-studied eloquence. Jackie relives what was arguably her finest hour.

'It was terrible what happened to Mandy and Beth. Those poor women had been terrorised by that brutal Trevor and when they tried to defend themselves, the court locked them up...with Mandy pregnant 'n' all. It was so unjust. When I heard that Pat Farnham and Jean Crosbie were organising a campaign to get the Jordaches out of jail, I was determined to do my bit.

'Being part of the campaign was really good for me. Marriage to Jimmy isn't always a bundle of laughs – he used to be on Crime Watch more than Nick Ross – but the campaign made me feel that for once in my life, I was doing something worthwhile. Pat was very much the organiser (self-appointed, if the truth be told), but with her PR experience, she was great at making sure we got as much publicity as possible. And Jean had

so much energy. I don't know what Bing was putting in her cocoa! Rosie Banks joined us too sometimes, even though Eddie was worried about her condition. Well, she was heavily pregnant.

'One of the first things we did was organise a candle-lit vigil on the steps of St. George's Hall. Ron and Bev didn't want to know. They said justice had been done and anyway it'd just be a load of lesbians with shaved heads. I've never worn a pair of dungarees in me life. It was ridiculous. That Bev is such a bigot, but I expected better from Ron. I think he's afraid to stand up to her.

'A photo of the vigil made the Echo, and Pat told us that one of the satellite TV stations had invited us along to appear on a special programme about domestic violence. Jimmy said I wanted to

NEIGHBOURS

Mal Young: 'We were planning to bring Jackie Corkhill into the show more. Sue Jenkins, who plays Jackie, is really believable as Jimmy's wife and we knew we would be involving Jackie in the drugs stories with Jimmy and with the return of their daughter Lindsey. But before we did that, we wanted the audience to get to know more about Jackie. We wanted to take her into other areas, away from the Corkhill family unit. We thought: "Let's hear her opinions on Mandy's plight; let's see her chat with Jean Crosbie, somebody with whom, on the face of it, she would appear to have little in common." The reaction to the Jordache story was incredible. We kept the outcome of the trial a secret and filmed two endings so that all of the cast and crew were kept in the dark. And we had to keep this up for seven weeks, to the point of shooting two versions of everything – one as if Mandy and Beth had been acquitted and were free, the other as if they had been found guilty and were in jail. The only people who knew the outcome were Phil Redmond and myself, and even I wasn't sure until the afternoon of transmission. I was half expecting Phil to twist it on me! We consulted real judges about the case and they said it was likely that the Jordaches would go down – especially Beth. So although the verdict disappointed some people, it was the most realistic. Besides, we realised that a conviction followed by an appeal would fuel further debate. After the case, the battered wives' group, Refuge, was swamped with calls for help from women in Mandy's situation and both the Metropolitan Police and the Home Office asked for copies of the programme tapes. The Met requested them to help train their officers dealing with domestic violence and the Home Office wanted to pass them on to probation officers having to deal with male offenders. So that was very gratifying. We even had an American news crew come over to report on the "Jordache phenomenon". They described Brookside as a cross between Dynasty and Cheers because they'd never seen anything like it in the States! Some people wondered why we killed off Beth. Well, we knew that Anna Friel (who played Beth) and Sandra Maitland (Mandy) were leaving the show that year and, other than escaping from jail, we knew there was no way that Beth was going to get out. We couldn't leave Beth languishing unseen in jail because people would want to know what was happening to her. Also Beth's death re-focused the story on Mandy's plight. We didn't want Beth, the lesbian icon, which was a separate story, getting in the way of the domestic violence debate.'

Pat Farnham wasn't keen on me joining the campaign, but I think I won her round.

be careful that Pat didn't hog the limelight and that I should make sure I went on the show too. I was made up at the thought of being on national TV. Eat your heart out, Cilla Black. In the meantime, Sinbad and Jean were sticking up 'The Jordaches Are Innocent' posters all over the city. Jean, in particular, seemed to be getting a real buzz out of breaking the law. She was well on her way to becoming an honorary Corkhill...

'When we got to the TV studios, I was put out when they said they only wanted two of us from

THE BROOKSIDE FILES

the campaign on. It was clear that Pat wanted Jean rather than me. She always did look down her nose at the Corkhills. Then again, she'd look down her nose at royalty. But Jean got cold feet at the last minute and so I took her place. Michael Parkinson was the presenter – he's still dead handsome, even better than in the Seventies – and the other guests were some MP and a professional wife-beater. Before the show, Parky warned us it might get a bit heated. He was right. I'm afraid I lost me rag listening to that smarmy MP going on about how the Jordaches shouldn't have taken the law into their own hands. What the hell did he know? Sitting on his fat majority in his smart detached house with his cocktail evenings and dinner parties. What did he

know about domestic violence and child abuse? What did he know about a mother's natural instinct to protect her daughter? He probably never experienced an emotion in his life. I shouted him down, saying that it was time he came into the real world. I quite forgot meself and felt dead awkward the moment I'd said it. But my embarrassment went when the audience started applauding. After the show, everyone came up to tell me how well I'd done. I was made up.

'I know Pat was getting a lot of hassle from Max about carrying on with the campaign, but Jimmy was dead good about it. In fact he was so

People told me that the TV show was my finest hour, but I only said what I felt.

nice I thought he must be up to something. Sure enough, he was torching some van yard and putting Carl Banks in hospital. It was just another day at the office for Jimmy.

'Our next publicity stunt was a darts marathon, but it didn't really work. The papers weren't interested. We needed something harder-hitting, a story to keep the Jordaches' names in the spotlight. Without publicity, our cause was hopeless. Jean and I mulled over a few ideas before coming up with a cracker. It was so good we daren't tell a soul. When the bell went at the end of our next prison visit to see Mandy and Beth, we got out some nylon cable and tied all our hands together. Mandy and Beth were stunned by the show of solidarity. We told the guard that we weren't leaving until we got justice for the Jordaches. There was a bit of a commotion and the guards bundled us out...into the lenses of the press photographers who we'd tipped off in advance. Jimmy and Bing were summoned to collect us. Jimmy was dead proud of me for pulling a fast one on the law.

'We got loads of coverage from that and decided to step up the campaign by staging a protest outside the prison gates. I rang round some women's groups and they said they'd come and support us. I thought, the more people we got involved, the better. Armed with our thermos flasks, we spent best part of a week outside the prison, day and night. Rosie Banks and Julia Brogan turned up to bolster our spirits with supplies of sandwiches. As more and more people arrived, a really good atmosphere built up. I was rallying support through this megaphone and at one point, Julia whipped it off me and started everyone off on a good old-fashioned

Our protest outside the prison was going well until rent-a-mob turned up and things turned nasty.

sing-song. I was really enjoying myself. The only black spot was Max Farnham. He was furious that Pat was on the demo – he was probably scared it would damage his public standing – and said she was neglecting the kids. He practically forced her to go home. At least my Jimmy would know better than to try anything like that with me.

'The police told us we were OK – we'd only be moved on if any trouble broke out. That was fine by us. All we wanted was a peaceful protest. But then Jean and I spotted coachloads of strangers turning up, like those travellers you see on the

Mandy Jordache's release made all our efforts worthwhile.

news. I didn't like the look of them, and nor did Jean. They looked as if they were out to cause trouble. More and more of them started arriving. I could feel I was losing control of the situation. The police warned me again that if there was any bother, they'd stop the protest. No sooner had they said that than the van carrying Mandy and Beth emerged from the gates. Word got around that the prison authorities had decided to move them to another prison, in Yorkshire, to try and cool things down. When this uninvited mob saw the van, they charged it and scuffles broke out. I was terrified and angry – this wasn't what our protest was about. This would do more harm than good. In the mêlée, Rosie Banks was knocked about a bit. As she sat down to get her breath back, the police thought she was a protestor and carted her off to the station. She ended up losing the baby. I felt really bad about it.

'After that, it was a question of waiting for the Court of Appeal date ... and hoping. Of course, the result was marred by Beth's tragic death. We'd come so far together and then at the final hurdle, she was struck down by a heart complaint. What a miserable last few months she had. Life really is a bitch, isn't it? Still at least Mandy was freed so our efforts were certainly not in vain. On the contrary, I hope we've inspired other women in the same situation.

'I think being involved in the Jordache campaign has made me a better person. It's certainly made me aware of what bastards some men are. Jimmy may have his faults, but he's never raised a finger to me. And I know if he ever did, I'd be out of that door like a shot.'

NEIGHBOURS

Julia Brogan on the Art of Discretion

Billy Corkhill's former mother-in-law Julia Brogan is Brookside's resident busybody. She knows everyone on the Close and is not afraid to air her views on their behaviour. Some people think she's an interfering old witch; others aren't sure about her age. Julia was only too happy to share with us her opinion of some of the residents who have slipped past her net curtains.

'Oh yes, I've seen 'em all, me. Murderers, rapists, robbers, arsonists – if you ask me, there's too much arson about in this day and age – wife-beaters, drug dealers, con-men. And most of them in the family my Doreen married into. Always up to no good, them Corkhills. But worst of all in my book are philatelists – I can't abide men who go chasing after women.

'Where shall I start? Close to home, I suppose. Jimmy Corkhill. He's an even bigger rogue than his brother. Lord knows, Billy had more fiddles than the Liverpool Philharmonic but nothing Jimmy would do surprises me. And he's always made it patently clear that I'm not welcome in his house. Well, I wouldn't soil me shoes by setting foot over his door. Anyway you go in there for a cup of tea and you're not sure whether you're getting two sugars or something which will lead to you having your stomach pumped out in hospital. The only trip I want to go on is one organised by Saga. And that poor little kiddie, stuck in jail out East somewhere just because her grandad's a druggie. They want locking up, the lot of them.

'Still, I'd rather Doreen had married a Corkhill than a Dixon. What a family. The only decent one was Ron's father, Cyril, but even he had a string

Mal Young: 'Gladys Ambrose, who plays Julia Brogan, has got tremendous energy and an amazing history. I've got this poster from the 1960s of her on the same bill as the Beatles and Ken Dodd. And Julia has got that same energy. So whenever a scene needs a bit of spark, along comes Julia. She's one of those rare characters who can go into anyone's shop or house. Some people will only knock on certain people's doors but Julia can go everywhere – not even to buy anything, just to talk. Also we wanted to portray a more positive image of older age – it's not all about senility, bed-wetting and going to funerals. A lot of retired people have a great time. Julia is a very positive character. Occasionally, we see a glimpse of her serious side, such as when her niece Diana was raped. Now Julia has taken over as the Farnhams' cleaner and becomes Susannah's confidante, I'm sure that Julia will cause even more sparks to fly in the Farnham household of women stretching from Bootle to Blackpool. Just when it looked as if I was getting him up the aisle, he went and died. Some men are so inconsiderate. As for Ron Dixon, I can still hardly bear to speak his name – not after that time he accused me of stealing from his shop. You wouldn't mind, but I was a good worker behind that counter – and very popular with the customers. Not that Ron cared about that – all he wanted was their money. He made Scrooge look like a charity-worker. Anyway, their Mike had been robbing from the till and Ron blamed me. I was going to sue him for character aspiration. I don't like that Bev either. She's got too much to say for herself, that one. As for her clothes, I've seen wounds better dressed. And that Jacqui's a cocky little madam. Barely tolerates me in the salon, she does. No manners. And she's got split ends.

The Simpsons were all smiles at first – but I knew it wouldn't last.

'I never took to the Farnhams either, apart from his new one – well, old one really – Susannah, who gave me a lovely lot of stuff for the over 55s auction and a cleaning job into the bargain. But that Pat always had a smell under her nose, as if she was doing you a favour just by saying hello, and he was nothing but a common kerb-crawler. All those airs and graces and he went round chasing women of the night. I know he was found not guilty, but as I always say, there's no fire without smoke. Mind you, you could understand where he got it from. You only have to look at his father-in-law, David Crosbie. Old enough to know better he is, but it doesn't stop him chasing after anything in a short skirt. And to think, I once held a candle for him. Now I know he's not even worth a candle!

'And what about the Jordaches? Husband buried under the patio, wife pregnant by the local window-cleaner and daughter preferring her own kind, if you know what I mean. Nobody's going to tell me that's normal. Still I did enjoy their trial, and I was able to finish the last few rows of my knitting.

'That Mick Johnson used to be a nice enough chap but he's gone a bit funny lately. I heard someone say he was on them stereothingies. And there's some odd rumours going around about the Simpsons. Not that I'm one to listen to idle chit-chat, you understand. They used to live in a big house in Formby and now they're on the Close. A bit of a fall from grace, that. There's something fishy if you ask me. It wouldn't surprise me to learn that they're international criminals on the run and are wanted by Interflora.

'I can't say I ever really got to know the Banks, but the way they left under a cloud, in the dead of night, said it all. She'd gambled away the lot. That's the trouble with those lotteries – they're always won by people who don't deserve large sums of money. If you ask me, they should give it all to the pensioners. But anyway, being neighbourly, I decided to pop in on the Banks' closing-down sale. It was poor quality stuff. You could see they weren't used to money. I bought a lampshade, but only out of pity, and when I got it home, it just didn't look right. You should have heard the fuss when I asked for me money back. I told 'em I never have that trouble at Marks and Sparks.

'I like to keep meself to meself. I've still got that Peter as a lodger. He's a nice lad, though I'm not sure yet whether he's a typical hairdresser...if you get my drift. And I was mortified over that business between him and Bev and Ron Dixon. When the ambulance pulled up to take Ron to hospital, all the neighbours started nosing. I didn't want people thinking I allowed any shenanigans under my roof.

'People often say to me: "Julia, what makes a good neighbour?" I tell them it's a matter of getting on with people, being broad-minded and remaining discreet at all times. It certainly works for me.'

Peter's a lovely hairdresser. I've told him he could be the next Vidal Bassoon.

THE BROOKSIDE FILES
RELATIONSHIPS

Mick Johnson on Jenny Swift

When he was young, Mick Johnson must have walked under a ladder one day, tripped over a black cat and smashed into a mirror. Never has one man had so much bad luck. He's lost his wife, his home, his girlfriend, been taken to court for apprehending a burglar and been wrongfully arrested for armed robbery on his wedding day. But this was nothing compared to the dramas that were to unfold when he met Jenny Swift.

'Even now, I hate talking about Jenny Swift. The way she screwed up her own life and tried to screw up mine. She's locked away now, but there's hardly a day goes by when I don't wonder whether she's been released. And if the phone rings and there's nobody there, I start thinking that she's coming back to get me. And make no mistake, she's mad enough to be capable of anything.

'It all started when I went to a school parents' evening and saw her about our Leo. She was Leo's teacher and seemed really friendly and enthusiastic. She wasn't bad looking either, but I wasn't interested in all that. Leo was having a few problems at the time – name-calling and that – and, after his mate Garry's death at the baths, he had become scared of the water. Jenny offered to take him for

Mal Young: 'We wanted to look at obsession. There had been a number of cases of stalkers in the United States which weren't infatuations with pop stars or movie stars, but with ordinary people, someone who was simply spotted in the street. And somehow that made it all the more chilling. It is a difficult area because the law is so flimsy on stalkers. I read of a case where one person had a court injunction against their stalker broken 150 times! We deliberately cast Kate Beckett as Jenny Swift because she looked so innocent. It was the same with casting Bryan Murray as Trevor Jordache and Andrew Fillis as Gary Stanlow. If we're looking for a villain, we don't go for stereotypes – we choose someone who looks positively angelic. And when we cast for a character who's going to turn out to be a baddie, we never tell the actor in advance because you don't want them playing it in their eyes, you want them playing it straight. That adds to the power of the performance.'

RELATIONSHIPS

My blood boils when I think what Jenny put me through.

swimming lessons after school, which I thought was really nice. Just to say thank you, I took her a box of chocolates. It was just an innocent gesture, like. If I'd known what it would lead to, I'd have put razor blades in the strawberry creams.

'After that, she sort of materialised wherever I went. She kept turning up at Pizza Parade and even wangled an invite to Rosie Banks's fortieth birthday party. That night, she said she was ill, so me being a gentleman, offered to run her home. When we got to her flat, she made an amazing recovery. She dragged me in for coffee, but I felt dead uncomfortable. I remember I went to the loo and when I came out, she was standing there starkers except for me jacket over her shoulders. I got out of that flat sharpish. She apologised the next day and I explained that I just wasn't ready for a relationship. I thought that would be the end of it.

'But still she seemed to be following me around all the time, more of a shadow than Hank Marvin. Bouquets of flowers and boxes of chocolates started arriving for me. And I was getting these crank phone calls in the shop. The phone would ring but there'd be nobody on the other end. Even then, I didn't really think she was

behind the calls – until, that is, I found that she'd told the world we were getting engaged. She'd even thrown a surprise party for me, inviting everyone on the Close. And there was this cake with 'Mick and Jenny' written on it. I threw a wobbler. I said there was no engagement and told her to get out. I never wanted to see her again. She was seriously deranged.

THE BROOKSIDE FILES

'I didn't want her teaching Leo any more – I wanted him moved to another class – but the headmaster wasn't interested. And still she was going round telling people we were getting married. I couldn't believe it. The trouble was, she looked so sweet and harmless, as if butter wouldn't melt in her mouth, that everyone believed her and liked her. I was made out to be the bad guy. It was only Sinbad and Sarah Banks who seemed to see through her. In desperation, I told her that I was already in a relationship...with Sarah. I couldn't think of any other way of putting her off. And the silent phone calls were doing me head in.

'I tried going to the police, but they wouldn't take me seriously. They said sending flowers and

I couldn't believe it when I saw all those photos of me in her bedroom.

chocolates wasn't a crime yet. I decided to take the kids up to Southport for a few days, just to get away from her, and Sinbad tagged along too. So did she – she followed us all the way up there. Back home, I got a solicitor to send her a letter, telling her to keep away, but she just seemed to dismiss it as if she couldn't understand what all the fuss was about.

'She was that unstable I was worried she was going to do something daft so when Leo said she hadn't turned up for school one day, me and Sinbad went round to her flat to check she was OK. The door was open, but she wasn't in. I got

RELATIONSHIPS

the shock of me life in her bedroom – the walls were plastered with photos of me. It was like a shrine. There was a shirt and a bottle of me aftershave that she'd nicked from my place and even a bag full of my rubbish. At last I thought I had proof that she was some mad stalker and went to the police. When we got back to the flat with P.C. Coban, Jenny was waiting for us, and all the photos and stuff had gone. She'd made a right mug out of me. I asked her why she was doing this to me and she broke down and said she had a brain tumour and just wanted her last moments to be happy. She was so convincing

---

When Jenny ended up in hospital I felt I had to keep her sweet.

that, even after all the strokes she'd pulled, I found myself half believing her. Then she phoned me, saying she couldn't live without me and was going to top herself. Sinbad and I raced round and there she was again, right as rain, announcing that she'd prepared lunch to celebrate our anniversary – eight weeks together. I lost me rag, started smashing her photos, trying to get it into her head that I had no feelings whatsoever for her. She threatened to throw herself off the landing outside her flat. Looking back, I should have let her get on with it, but I tried to stop her. As I did so, the banister snapped and she plunged to the floor. Her landlady was looking at me, accusingly, but I hadn't done anything. It was all like a horrible dream.

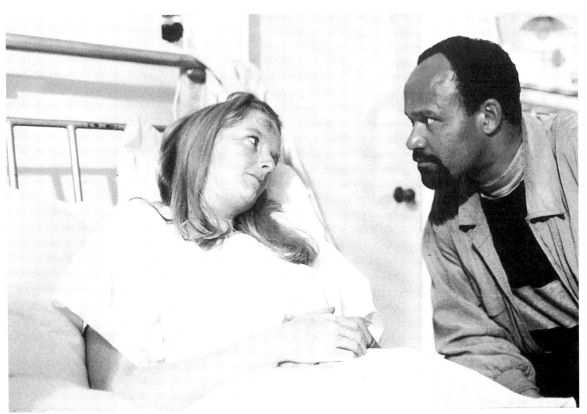

THE BROOKSIDE FILES

'The trouble was, Jenny could have told the police anything. I couldn't risk that, so I went to visit her in hospital, to keep her sweet. She told me she didn't blame me for pushing her and admitted that she'd probably driven me to it. I told her I hadn't touched her, but I was wasting my time. Then I found out from the neurologist that there was no brain tumour, but she came out with another sob story about her mum and dad being dead and how she needed someone to cling to. I know I'm soft, but I couldn't help feeling a bit sorry for her. It was a big mistake.

'She agreed to see a counsellor, but only if I went along to give her moral support. I couldn't just wash me hands of her, so I agreed. Just when I thought we were actually making some progress, she was evicted from her flat. She had nowhere to live and I was worried it might set her back, so I said she could stay with me...just until she found somewhere. Sinbad thought I was as mad as her. I think he had a point. Of course, once she'd settled herself in to my place, there was no shifting her. It was easier to get rid of dry rot. I kept dropping heavy hints, but they fell on stony ground. She promised me she'd move out any day and that she was really looking hard for a flat, but I had my doubts. And when me little girl Gemma asked whether Jenny was going to be her new mummy, I knew enough was enough. I had to make Jenny see once and for all that there was no future for us so I started dating Janice, a friend of Bev's. She was a good laugh and after nearly three months of Jenny, that was something I badly needed. Unbeknown to me, Jenny had been spying on us. Racked with jealousy, she went to Nottingham to see her dad (who,

needless to say, was still very much alive) and pinched a gun and some bullets from him.

'It was the day of Sinbad and Mandy's wedding and I was supposed to be best man. I was made up for Sinbad but more important to me was the fact that Jenny was supposed to be moving out that day. But as I went to say goodbye and head off for the register office, she got all emotional about never seeing me again and suddenly pulled the gun on me. At that stage, I didn't know whether it was real or not, but I wasn't prepared to take any chances.

'Three days she held me hostage. I tried reasoning with her, but she'd suddenly flare up again. I was terrified that she'd use the gun – either on herself or me. At one point, she dozed off and I tried to sneak out, but she woke up. She was crazy. Obviously people were wondering what had happened to me – it's not often the best man doesn't turn up for the wedding – and fortunately they informed the police. P.C. Coban came round to check that I was alright, only to find himself taken hostage too. At least he now knew I wasn't making it all up about Jenny. Then there was a commotion outside the door and in the struggle, she shot Ian Coban in the arm. She became crazier than ever, threatening to kill us all. I'd had enough of trying to placate her so I set about winding her up instead. I accused her of being nothing more than an attention seeker. Her eyes were wild with rage but it was enough to distract her and I was able to grab her, just as three armed police officers burst into the flat.

'I thought with her in custody, my worries were over, but she started laying the blame on me. The police said she could be out again if she was granted bail. I could see the whole nightmare

RELATIONSHIPS

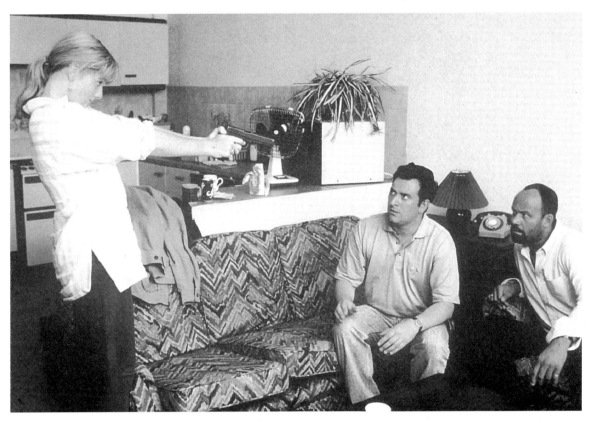

Nobody believed me when I said Jenny was crazy – until she held me and PC Coban hostage.

starting over again. I was really angry and bitter, even more so when she appeared in court for her bail application. Her father tried to make out that it was all my fault, that I must have driven his darling daughter to behave in the way she did. Luckily, she was refused bail.

'But still she was able to get to me. She phoned me from prison, wrote to me from prison, telling me how she'd be seeing me soon. Couldn't they stop her? It was me who was the prisoner, not her. I was really starting to crack up. I was scared stiff she'd get to Leo and Gemma so I kept them off school and taught them at home. Any strange car I saw near the Parade, I thought it must be her. The flat became a fortress. I put extra security locks on the door and hardly ventured out. It was even

worse for Leo and Gemma. They were just kids and needed to see their friends, but Jenny had got me so mixed up I was frightened to let them out of my sight. It got too much for Leo one night and he and Gemma crept off to sleep in Jimmy Corkhill's Korky Cars caravan. I was frantic with worry. I thought Jenny had managed to get them, even though I knew she was behind bars. I just wasn't thinking straight. When Ron Dixon brought them back, I was so angry at the pain they'd put me through that I lashed out at Leo – something I'd never done before. The moment I'd done it, I felt really bad about it. I said I was so sorry but Leo backed away. It was a few days before we were mates again.

'The build-up to her trial seemed to go on forever. She even had the nerve to write to me again, begging me to help her. No way. I just wanted her locked up for a long time. I was sure she'd walk free, particularly when her dad, who seemed almost as mad as her, got up in the witness box and said that it was all my fault. But Sinbad told me not to worry – she'd go down.

Thank God Jenny Swift is locked up now – but for how long?

He was right. She got three years, but as the judge passed sentence, she screamed that she'd get me. It really put the wind up me, I can tell you. I wasn't taking any chances. I wanted to move somewhere she wouldn't be able to find me. I actually thought about getting right out of Liverpool but Sarah Banks, who was renting number five on the Close, was happy to do a swap. So she moved in to the flat and me and Sinbad moved on to the Close. I feel a lot safer there, but I know one day I'll have to face the fact that she'll be free. Somehow I don't think I'll ever be completely rid of her.'

RELATIONSHIPS

Ron Dixon on Keeping a Younger Woman Happy

When the Simpsons first moved on to the Close, Bel immediately jumped to the conclusion that Ron Dixon was Bev's father. With an age difference of nigh on 30 years, it is an understandable mistake. Here Ron reveals the secret of keeping a younger woman happy.

'When I first got together with Bev, what was it three years ago, people thought I was mad. I had a good wife, three lovely kids, nice little house, me own business and I was risking everything for a girl half me age. But I felt I was growing old before me time. I suppose I was having a mid-life crisis – you know, when you start trying to recapture your youth by wearing fancy shirts, listening to Oasis CDs and leaving yer bedroom a tip. Like I say, DD's a good woman but not even the president of her fan club would say she's the life and soul of the party. She's always been more into Hail Marys than Bloody Marys. It had got to the stage where her and me just were plodding along towards the day I retired. I knew it was bad when she bought me a cardie one Christmas and one of them herbal baths for people with rheumatic backs. I thought, next she'll be buying me a mug for me teeth.

'So Bev was like a breath of fresh air. She was so...uninhibited. Sure, she's got more front than Blackpool, and a mouth that could swallow the Mersey Tunnel at times, but she's fun and she made me feel young again. I was finally able to use up that bottle of Hai Karate. It made me feel good, having a young girl like Bev on me arm. You know, flattering like. You could see blokes thinking: "He must have something to pull a cracker like that."

Mal Young: 'A few years ago, Irene Marot, who plays DD Dixon, wanted to take six months off from the show. We didn't want to lose Ron so we needed to give him something to do while DD was away. We discussed the possibility of him falling for a younger woman and decided that all the signs were there that he was on the lookout. Around that time, we saw an actress named Sarah White who'd just left drama school. We thought she was very interesting and so we cast her as this wild girl. To be honest, the Bev of today is nothing like we'd originally imagined. We'd have considered her to be too comical, too over the top. But it works. Together with the writers, Sarah has developed this amazing character. She's introduced the ear-rings, the leggings, the tight tops, the lot. Just like the neighbours, we didn't think their relationship would last this long, but Ron and Bev are really popular, particularly with youngsters. And of course the rivalry with DD is great. But we don't know what the future may hold. Ron and Bev's age gap will get bigger. As he slips quickly into old age, she's not going to age as fast and that could eventually drive them apart.'

Sometimes I felt more like Bev's dad when we went out.

'Of course, it's been a difficult few years, what with the fuss over Josh, our Tony being murdered by Corkhill and our Michael being banged up in Thailand. No wonder I had a heart attack. But I reckon that was probably brought on as much as anything by my own insecurity. That's the only drawback with having a young partner – at the back of your mind, there's always the fear that they're going to go off with someone their own age.

'That's why I got so uptight about Bev and that hairdresser Peter, the queen of the blow wave. I didn't like her working at the salon with him – he was a bad influence. She started staying out all hours, going clubbing and that, and wearing them bin-liner trousers. Hard to believe I know, but suddenly the Legion wasn't exciting enough for her. She said she was going out with her mates

but I later found out that she was seeing him behind me back, although I believe her when she said nothing happened. I think for her it was just a bit of fun, a chance to boogie on down or whatever it is they do these days. I suppose the last person you want in a throbbing nightclub is somebody with a dodgy ticker, and I have to admit my breakdancing's not what it was.

'At least I thought she still fancied me. In fact she was as demanding as ever – a bit too demanding for someone in my state of health. But I managed to do what a man's gotta do until I saw that she'd had her navel pierced. It was really revolting – like a ring-pull on a can of beer – and quite put me off me stroke. Turned out it was another of Peter's bright ideas. He had a lot to answer for.

'Then I discovered from the Liverpool Echo, Julia Brogan, that Bev had been helping Peter move into a room in Julia's house. And Bev had told me she was out with Avril that night. I'm afraid the green-eyed monster got the better of me. I followed her round there and saw her kiss him. I could feel me heart pounding away. I felt so betrayed – I thought she really loved me. But they say there's no fool like an old fool.

'I was fuming but she came back bold as brass and suddenly asked me to marry her. Almost in the same breath, she suggested that I make a will, leaving everything to her and Josh. I thought, I know your game, lady. You're after bumping me off and claiming half the Trading Post. It seemed that all along, she'd only been after me money.

'I'm ashamed to say I got paranoid. In fact, we could have done with one of them instant cameras. Instead I got our Michael to bug Peter's room so I could hear what was going on. It confirmed all me worst fears. I heard him telling Bev that Ron had had his day and served his purpose and that they could dispose of me when she'd finished with me. They even started joking about burying me under the patio, like that Jordache lot. Of course, it turned out that the Ron they'd been talking about

was a hairdresser's dummy that Bev had been practising on (Peter was giving her lessons), but I wasn't to know that, was I?

'I watched everything she gave me over the next few days, convinced that she was trying to poison me. When her chicken, Kiev, keeled over after eating some of the casserole which was meant for me, even Michael was beginning to come round to my way of thinking. I went round there, spoiling for a fight, but just as I was about to land Peter one, I suddenly felt these terrible pains in me chest. Next thing I knew I was lying in bed in hospital. Everyone had thought I was a goner – they'd even put me death notice in the paper – and apparently I had actually stopped breathing for two whole minutes. I was technically dead for that time. It's strange because I remember dying. I could see meself on the bed getting further away down a long dark tunnel. I even met Frank Rogers. It was like one of those out-of-body experiences that you read about in women's magazines. I thought, perhaps there

I was sure that Bev and Peter were plotting against me.

really was something on the other side – and I didn't mean Birkenhead.

'The experience left me at peace with the world. I even thought about removing the needles from me Jimmy Corkhill doll! I seriously considered letting Bev go, that maybe I was too much of a burden on her, but she was horrified that I could think of such a thing. She told me how much she loved me, that she didn't want to lose me and that she was committed to me for life. That meant a lot. But I knew if I was going to

The doctors told me I actually died after me heart attack.

stick around for a few more years I was going to have to take things easier. That's why Ronald Dixon, 'grocer', decided to retire. I wanted to make Jackie Corkhill manager at the Trading Post – she's always been a good worker, unlike the rest of her family – but Bev had her heart set on the job too. I didn't want to upset either of them, so I sorted out two envelopes and said whoever's got the one marked X has got the job. I thought I knew which was which but I got in a muddle and ended up handing the envelope with the cross to Bev by mistake. She was over the proverbial moon, so I couldn't back down. But I felt sorry for Jackie.

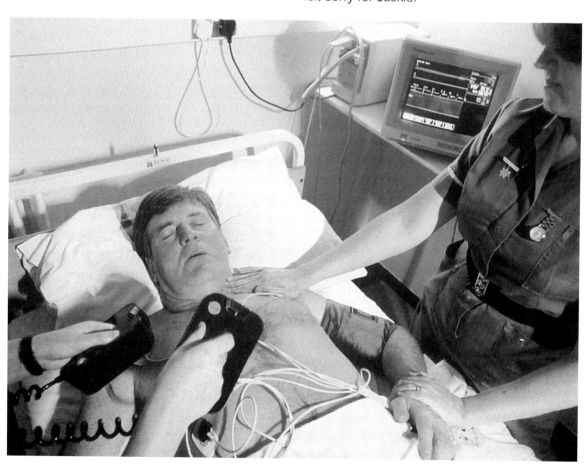

'Bev and I are really happy now, what with our Michael being released and engaged to Lindsey, even if she is a Corkhill. I'll admit there have been times over the past couple of years when I've wondered whether I made a mistake leaving DD for Bev. At times of crisis – and God knows, there've been plenty of those – Dee has always been there for me, despite all the hurt I know I've caused her. I used to hate it when she and Bev would start slagging each other off like a pair of fishwives. I think it was because Bev knew that Dee and I still felt something for each other and was just as insecure as I had been about her and Peter. But now DD's got a fella of her own, she's no threat to Bev.

'Bev's been good for me, and I like to think I've been good for her, although I do seem to spend a

Bev's feuding with DD brought me nothing but misery.

lot of me time going round after her, trying to smooth over people that she's upset. I feel like the bloke with the dustpan and brush at the Horse of the Year Show. I'm not so possessive now. I let her have her freedom cos it's only to be expected that she sometimes wants to meet people her own age. By giving her that, I find she doesn't take advantage of me. In fact, I've only got one complaint – and that's her bloody vegetarian cooking. I'm just hoping some scientist comes up soon with a Mad Nut Cutlet Disease so we can get back to a nice leg of lamb for Sunday lunch. That would be heaven. And don't forget, I know – I've already been there.'

THE BROOKSIDE FILES

Sinbad on Keeping Two Women on the Go

Sinbad has never been lucky in love. First Marcia Barrett then Mandy Jordache left him in the lurch. But this summer he found himself in the enviable position of having two fiancees at the same time. Women just couldn't leave him alone. So how did a humble window-cleaner suddenly become the Tom Cruise of Brookside Close?

'For years, women treated me like I have the plague. I made stomachs turn rather than heads. But just recent like, everything's suddenly started coming up roses for me. I seem to have become irresistible to the opposite sex. At first, I put it down to me new bucket, but it seems they want me for me mind – even me body. Medical science will have to wait.

'Actually, it was Mick's body that started it all off – not that I'm going funny, like, but him and me began working out. It's funny when people say they want to keep in shape, they never mean my shape. Anyway Jackie Corkhill's sister, Val, got chatting to Mick about the size of his pectorals and that, and it turned out that she did a bit of body-building. I bet she thought my body was built by Wimpey but we got on OK and Mick said I should ask her out. I thought she was out of my league, but when you're in the same league as Skelmersdale United, what can you expect. Mick fancied her himself and was secretly hoping to cop off with her, but she told him it was me she was after. You should've seen his face. He looked like he'd swallowed a lemon.

Mal Young: 'Sinbad first came in as a happy-go-lucky scally window-cleaner, sharing a few gags with Jimmy Corkhill, but it was interesting to take them on a series of adventures away from comedy. We deliberately put Sinbad into the Jordache story because we wanted the audience to have a representative in there. Sinbad is Everyman, Mr. Ordinary. Then we decided that he'd had a heavy two years with digging up bodies and court cases so we wanted to give him a bit of light relief. What better way than to have two women chasing after him? The more serious side of his story is that he reaches 40 in January 1997 and he wants to be settled down with a wife and a family. He is looking for happiness and normality in his life.

He represents a part of our audience who leave getting married and having children till later in life. Research tells us that these days more single people than ever are getting married in their late thirties and early forties, and that brings on a set of potential new problems. So, on the rebound from Mandy, Sinbad is in a rush to settle down and feels that he has to get married before he's 40. He wants children but of course his future wife might not be able to have them at her age. It's a fascinating area to explore and one which is relevant to many people.'

RELATIONSHIPS

'I took so long deciding whether or not to ask her out that in the end she did it for me. Usually if a woman made the first move with me, it was towards the door. We were going for a quiet romantic dinner for two at Grants. I spent all day getting ready. I dusted down me best suit and even washed behind me ears. I was dead nervous, but she said she'd heard that flares were making a comeback. The way I felt they were distress flares. But we sat down to eat and everything was fine until Peter the hairdresser turns up with some new girl he'd just taken on called Fee. We'd have had more privacy on the Kop on a Saturday afternoon.

'A couple of days later, this Fee, who, it turns out, is Peter's sister, calls into me new shop and says she wants a second-hand tumble dryer for the salon. She wanted to know whether it'd been in for a service recently, but I said I didn't think it was even religious. Anyway, no sooner had she got it than it went wrong, but as I was fixing it, I felt me back go. She insisted I take me shirt off while she gave me a massage. The tumble dryer wasn't the only thing that was stripped down to its parts.

'Next thing I realise, she fancies me an' all. I thought, I'm gonna wake up in a minute. Since it was Wimbledon fortnight, she dragged me off for a game of tennis and a picnic. Now the last time I played tennis, Fred Perry was Britain's number one. But even though me whites wouldn't have been chosen for any washing powder commercials, we had a good laugh. Trouble was when I got home, Val was waiting for me, asking whether I'd forgotten about our date. I was knackered but she wouldn't take no for an answer and whisked me off to ballroom dancing lessons. By the end, I definitely felt I'd been tangoed!

It was a good job Val did the chasing – I'd never have caught up with her!

'From then on, it was a case of keeping Fee and Val apart. It was like one of them old Brian Rix farces. Whenever I went to me wardrobe to get a shirt, I was never sure whether I'd find a woman hiding there. When Val took me off on holiday I had to tell Fee I was going down to Bristol to look after Ruth for a while. I came back with the sort of tan you don't normally get on the Avon. I'd had a great time with Val, but the moment I was back, I couldn't wait to go away with Fee. So I went off with Fee for a bit – if you know what I mean – and told Val I was going down to Bristol to look after Ruth! The thing was, I enjoyed being with them both – but not together – and as long as they were both happy, I didn't see why I had to choose between them. It was like being one of them blokes off Blind Date, except I didn't get made to look a divvy.

'But a few days after I'd got back off me second holiday, I nearly got the shock of me life. There was Val in the salon, having her nails done by Fee. They were both talking about their holidays – which, let's face it, is all you ever do talk about at the hairdresser's – and Fee was about to get her holiday snaps out. Fortunately I managed some story to get Val out in time, but it was a close shave, certainly closer than you get at that place. Jimmy said Jackie would go spare if she found out I was doing the dirty on her sister. It was time I made a choice...well, soon anyway.

'Fee and me took Mick Johnno's kids to a theme park in the school holidays, and little Gemma kept calling Fee 'Val'. She wasn't the only one who was confused. Luckily Fee didn't suspect a thing. Just when I found meself getting closer to Fee – literally, 'cos she'd moved into the flat next to the salon – Val started complaining that she hadn't seen much of me since I got back from Bristol. She said she still had strong feelings for me and was looking for a long-term commitment, like.

'By now I was coming up with so many tall stories, I was thinking of changing me name to Aesop. I had every excuse known to British Rail...and a few more. But Val was determined to pin me down – with her biceps, I wasn't going to argue – and invited me to Grants. To be honest, I thought she was going to break it off, but instead she said 'cos it was leap year, she was asking me to marry her. You could have knocked me down with a souffle. I accepted on the spot and David Crosbie brought over a bottle of free bubbly. It

RELATIONSHIPS

Fee was a great laugh but I couldn't go on stringing her along forever.

THE BROOKSIDE FILES

Are you watching, Pele? Me and Fee had a great day out with Gemma and Leo.

was dead romantic. I thought if I get free bubbly, I'll get engaged every day. Little did I know...

'Later, I told Mick the good news. He was made up for me, but told me how lucky I'd been that neither of my harem had twigged that I'd been two-timing them. He said I'd best go round and tell Fee that it was all off.

'The thing is, I've never been much cop at making speeches. I get nervous if I have to speak to directory enquiries. So all me words started coming out wrong. I must have sounded like Stanley Unwin. The upshot was, I thought I was letting her down gently and she thought I was proposing. Before I could explain, she told me she felt exactly the same way and had been

waiting for the right moment. Now she decided this was the right moment, and asked me to marry her. My gob has never been so smacked. Instinctively, I said yes. What else could I say? I really like her.

'So I had two fiancees, and I didn't know which one to choose. I thought about tossing a coin or being married to them on alternate days, or even catching the next bus for South America, but in the end I decided that Val was the woman I wanted to spend the rest of me life with. I hated letting Fee down, but that's the trouble with being a male sex symbol. Someone has to get hurt.

'I'm hitting the dreaded four-o in January so all I've got to do now is persuade Val to get hitched by then. What a pressie that would be. It would certainly make a change from the usual socks and aftershave.'

THE BROOKSIDE FILES
SEX

Nat Simpson on Relationships

When they first arrived on the Close, the Simpsons seemed to be a perfectly normal family, albeit one having to grow accustomed to living in reduced circumstances. The big event was to be the wedding of Nat Simpson to Jules Bradley, but there was one major obstacle to Nat tying the knot...his incestuous relationship with his older sister Georgia. Nat looks back on the summer of discontent.

'I can't pretend that there was ever much parental blessing for Jules and me. Mum felt we were too young and that I was rushing into things with a girl I hardly knew. I suppose she had a point – we had only been together five months. Deep down, I wasn't even sure whether I wanted it. Maybe it was like joining the

Foreign Legion. I was getting married to forget. As ever, dad was his usual laid-back self, happy to let me do what he thought I wanted. But I could tell that neither he nor mum cared much for the Bradleys, particularly Jules's father, J.C., who went about things like a bull in a china shop. For their part, Jules's parents were rather surprised to find that we were living in a much smaller house than the one we'd had in Formby. They had hoped that their daughter was marrying into money. Now they weren't so sure. Also, I just wanted a quiet register office wedding but the Bradleys insisted we have the full works in

church. I'm amazed they didn't book a choir.

'I think the strain of all the preparations was getting to Jules and me, but that was nothing to the bombshell when Georgia turned up unannounced one evening. We hadn't spoken for six months – not since the night before she married Martin. It had been the longest six months of my life, trying to come to terms with the fact that she was enjoying sex with someone else and not me. The only way I could blot it out, I thought, was to find a steady girlfriend of my own. Something was now obviously wrong between Georgia and Martin because she asked if she could stay over for a while. My heart told me it was great to see her again – she looked fantastic – but my head told me it was something I really didn't need, not when I was about to get married.

'She slept downstairs on the sofa but in the middle of the night, I went down for a glass of water. She told me how much she missed me,

THE BROOKSIDE FILES

Mal Young: 'The incest story started life a couple of years ago at a long-term planning meeting with Phil Redmond when we were looking at the whole area of sexuality. The original idea was for a happy, loving young couple to move on to the Close and for them to turn out to be brother and sister. But it didn't have as much power as we wanted because it didn't affect enough people. The neighbours would be shocked, but so what? A year later, we knew we wanted to bring in a middle-class family to balance things up. We had lots of working-class families on the Close but we'd lost Patricia and Jean so we needed a friend for Max and Susannah. We thought: "Where better for this new family to move into than between the Corkhills and the Dixons?" We began to develop the Simpsons and it quickly became apparent that we could use the brother and sister story in there. Like the Jordaches, the Simpsons came in with a bang – and plenty of secrets. We've portrayed the incest in a dark, dangerous way. The audience have been in on it from day one, waiting for Nat and Georgia's secret to be exposed. People expected them to be revealed as half-brother and sister, thinking that's the way we'll cop out, but Brookside can't cop out. The first reaction from the writers to the incest storyline was a bit blase. After the Jordaches, they didn't think it was anything remarkable. It's another slow-burner but it could turn out to be just as big. Having said that, on Brookside we have to make sure that we're not constantly trying to top our last big story. You have to take a few steps back and come up with good stories which may not necessarily be bigger and more sensational than the last, just different and relevant to the audience. Trying to come up with something more sensational is a dangerous game because you'll end up with aliens landing on the Close! I remember people saying how we'd never top the first siege in 1985 when Kate Moses died. It was the same when Sheila Grant was raped, when Damon died and when Billy and Sheila left. But Brookside moves on and the audience move on with it. I'm glad when people say Brookside isn't like it was back in 1982. It shouldn't be. It has to reflect life in 1996.'

how sorry she was that we'd fallen out because we used to be so close. I said that was precisely the reason why she should have stayed away. I asked her why she'd suddenly come back and she said it was because she had heard that I'd brought the wedding day forward. She had to come back and see me, she said. She didn't want me to rush into things like she had. I went back to bed and Jules, my mind in a turmoil.

'Jules started quizzing me about Georgia, particularly when Georgia appeared, half-naked, with breakfast in bed for us. I said our row was all in the past and that I didn't really want to talk about it. I'd got enough on my plate, what with upcoming architecture exams.

Georgia was always on my mind.

SEX

'I tried to avoid being left alone in the house with Georgia. I knew I couldn't trust myself. But somehow she always managed to get me on my own. She pulled me close to her. I tried to hold back, but it was no use. We kissed passionately. She knew that when it came to the crunch, I couldn't help myself. She told me she thought I was making a big mistake marrying Jules, but I could see that she just didn't want to lose me.

Poor Jules – she had no idea what was going on.

'A few days later, she returned announcing that she'd left Martin. Again, I tried to tell her our relationship was over and must stay that way, but she could tell I didn't really mean it. The atmosphere in the house was so tense whenever we were in the room together, all the more when mum and dad, who obviously knew nothing of our affair, insisted that we hug and make up. Living under the same roof as Georgia was driving me insane. It got to the point where I suggested to Jules that we elope together now, rather than wait until August to get married. I'd convinced myself that if Jules and I were married, Georgia would be forced to leave us alone. But Jules dismissed the idea after discussing it with her new friend...Georgia.

'Sex between me and Jules had never been that good since we came to the Close. Everything was so cramped – I felt the rest of the family could hear our every move. And now with Georgia on my mind, it was well nigh impossible. I just couldn't focus on having sex with Jules when the person I really wanted to be with was in another room. Worse still, Jules went and told Georgia that I had gone off sex. I didn't want her knowing about our personal problems. No matter how much

THE BROOKSIDE FILES

pain it would cause me, I decided the only way for us to lead normal lives was to effect a reconciliation between her and Martin, but she wouldn't hear of it. She said she wanted me, not Martin. What on earth was I going to do?

'Georgia was testing my emotions – my real emotions. She suddenly declared that she couldn't bear the mental torture of being with me, but not being able to have me. She was going to find a place of her own and would come back and see me after the wedding. She told me she couldn't cope with watching me marry Jules, that it would break her heart. I was sure – and secretly hoped – that she didn't really mean it. I thought she was waiting to see what my reaction would be.

'She did move out, but sneaked back on to the Close to see Susannah Farnham. I was missing her like crazy so when I saw her car, I knew I had to follow her, to find out where she was living. I had tried to convince myself that all my feelings for Georgia were in the past, but I clearly had to start facing up to reality. She wanted me and I wanted her. Where that left Jules, I didn't know. I suggested that maybe we should postpone the wedding. Jules was shocked and confused. She said she couldn't wait to walk down the aisle with me. The stress really hit me at the wedding rehearsal. I completely flipped and ended up marching out of the church, leaving Jules stranded at the altar. Perhaps it was an omen she should have heeded.

'I knew Georgia had gone to stay at our grandfather's cottage in the Cotswolds. I had to be there with her. At first, she wasn't too pleased to see me – she said she had been trying to keep out of the way, to let me get on with my life. But I just couldn't keep away, I was infatuated with her.

We talked and talked, attempting to make sense of it all, searching for a solution. No matter how much we both wanted to, there was no way we could continue with the relationship – apart from anything else, incest is against the law. Who knew what might happen to us if we were discovered! And I knew we wouldn't be able to keep it a secret forever. If mum and dad ever found out, it would destroy them. And what about Jules? I couldn't break her heart by pulling out of the wedding. I knew I'd have to go back to Liverpool and go through with it. As far as I was concerned, it was the end for me and Georgia. But when I went to kiss her goodbye, all my emotions surged to the surface. I kissed her like I never kiss Jules. Georgia responded and persuaded me that we should have sex one last time. Even if I had wanted to, I was powerless to resist. It was as wonderful as ever – I had almost forgotten how good sex with Georgia was. At that point, Max Farnham, who to our acute embarrassment was also staying at the cottage with his ex-wife and their children, walked in on us. Our secret was out.

'I got back to Liverpool the day before the wedding. I was a bag of nerves in case the Farnhams spilled the beans. I tried to defuse the situation by telling them that we were only step-brother and sister and begged them not to tell my parents. Besides, I said, it was all over now. I also had to make it up with Jules. I apologised for running out of the church like that and promised that everything would be OK. She forgave me. She really is a nice girl. She'd make somebody a wonderful wife.

'The wedding day seemed to last an eternity. My heart wasn't in it at all. Dad, to his credit,

SEX

realised something still wasn't quite right. He said I didn't have to go through with it. He gave me a chance, but I wasn't brave enough to take it. I thought the only way to get through the day was to get blind drunk. To add to my confusion, Georgia turned up out of the blue. She had promised she wouldn't. Jules and I didn't even sleep together on our wedding night. I crashed

We talked and talked in the Cotswolds, but nothing made sense.

out in a chair while she sobbed herself to sleep. I'd ruined her big day. She deserved someone better than me. The next morning, she virtually tried to force me to have sex. It wasn't an unreasonable request – we were man and wife for

God's sake – but I just couldn't and backed away. Poor Jules ran downstairs in tears and told everyone the marriage was over.

'Needless to say, there was a big family inquest with both sides trying to decipher my behaviour. In my absence, they'd obviously decided I must be gay – something guaranteed to make J.C.'s hackles rise. When I appeared, dad quietly asked me whether I was gay. If I denied it, I knew I'd have to come up with another explanation for my physical rejection of Jules. I said nothing and just then, Georgia came to my rescue by telling them they'd drive me to a nervous breakdown if they kept on at me like that. However, my failure to deny that I was gay was clearly taken as an admission. My parents were very supportive, saying that they'd never guessed I was gay, but would help me in whatever way they could. I'd have preferred it if they'd started shouting at me – sometimes mum and dad's liberal cosseting gets on my nerves. Later, Georgia got me on my own. She said I should "come out" so that we could use my fake

homosexuality as a cover for living together. No one would suspect a thing. It was very tempting.

'A couple of days later, J.C. – he actually behaves like he's Jesus Christ – came round to say that he'd consulted a solicitor about annulling the marriage. Since it was never consummated, he had a good case. I decided to tell Jules I was gay. She was dreadfully hurt, but it seemed easier – kinder even – than telling her the truth.

I was powerless to resist Georgia. I wanted her so much.

SEX

Our wedding was a sick joke. I'm still sorry that I upset Jules.

'But nobody seemed to believe me – my mother, my father, not even Jules. She refused to accept that I was gay. She knew how good our sex life had been in Formby and couldn't understand why it was suddenly different. And all the time there was her bloody father dividing up the wedding presents. I couldn't take it, and nor could she. In fact, she got so fed up with her old man that she left home and moved into the house

he had bought her and me as a wedding present. And that only caused further complications because who went and moved in with her? Georgia.

'My life is a total wreck. I can't spend any time alone with Georgia because my wife's there. And my wife thinks the reason I went off her was because I've been having an affair with Susannah Farnham. She based this ridiculous deduction on the fact that she saw me in a cafe with Susannah. I've lost everything and everyone. I just don't know which way to turn.'

THE BROOKSIDE FILES

Bev McLoughlin on Undergoing Tests to Determine the Father of Josh

Beverley McLoughlin was having an affair with shopkeeper Ronald Dixon. When Ron's wife DD found out, Bev took up with his son Michael instead. Nine months later, she gave birth to baby Josh. But who was the father? Bev explains her novel solution to the predicament.

It would all have been fine but for DD, the interfering old cow. Ron was chuffed to bits at being a dad again – I mean at his age he was happy to let people know he could still rise to the occasion. To all the neighbours, he was one step away from cardigan man. They thought his idea of a bit on the side was an extra portion of chips. But he was like a man possessed in that stock room – a sudden run on tinned pineapple chunks couldn't have got him more excited. As for Mike, I didn't think he was bothered about babies and that. He still had plenty of wild oats to sow. I really wanted Josh to be Ron's baby because I really loved Ron. Mike's a nice lad but he was just a bit of fun. So even though I couldn't be sure who the father was, saying it was Ron's seemed to keep everyone happy. Except DD, that is. I don't think modern technology's come up with an invention that could make her happy. She could win the lottery and

look miserable, though not as miserable as Rosie Banks a few weeks after her win.

'Anyway DD sees this daft video Mike made where he says Josh might be his son and that does it. From then on, she's going around all self-righteous like a cross between Mother Theresa and the Singing Nun, insisting that I have a blood test so she can lord it saying 'we are a grandmother'. I told her to mind her own business, but she said it was her business. She's got such a gob on her – I could've landed her one. She went and showed Ron leaflets about DNA tests or something. Poor Ron, he was so hen-pecked you could see the beak marks. But he said have the test just so we could get DD off our backs. I'd rather have got her off the planet. When Mike and Ron agreed to go for tests, I wasn't left with much choice. I kept telling Ron that Josh was definitely his son, but I think I was really just trying to convince myself. I

Mal Young: 'As with the Down's Syndrome story, we were keen to show how technology had moved on and how DNA testing can be used to determine the identity of a baby's father. Also by making Mike the father of Bev's baby, we knew that it would give us plenty of emotional baggage for the future, because that child remains Mike's and it's a ticking timebomb. Although Ron really strives to bring up Josh as his own, deep down inside he knows it's not his son, and this is the sort of situation which we can exploit in the future.'

SEX

It was hard work keeping Ron's mail from him.

was dead scared. Then Jackie Corkhill came up with a brilliant idea. She said why don't I go for the test – secret, like – but pretend to the others that I haven't. That way, if I didn't like the result, I could keep it quiet.

'So I told Ron I wasn't going. He threw a wobbly at first but I managed to sweet-talk him round, lying through me teeth that I didn't want to put Josh through all the turmoil. Fellas will believe anything. But still there was saint DD, sticking her oar in like the Oxford boat race crew, saying it just proved I was scared of finding out the truth.

'The only problem was I knew the results would be sent to Ron so I had to get to the enve-lope before him. One thing I did learn by opening Ron's mail was that he dyed his hair. Who'd have

thought that beneath that auburn mane he's really the colour of Desert Orchid!

'When the real letter came, I could hardly bear to open it. When it said that Mike was Josh's father, I was gobsmacked. I knew if Ron ever found out, that would be the end for him and me. Then Jackie had another of her bright ideas – God knows how she ever got to be a Corkhill – saying that if I had Ron's baby for real, there was no way he could leave me. So for the next few weeks I was all over Ron like a rash. He didn't know what had hit him. We put on more perfor-mances than The Mousetrap – first thing in the

THE BROOKSIDE FILES

Ron – bless him – has always thought of Josh as his own.

morning, last thing at night and any time in between when he came up for air. It was all too much for the poor old thing. Even his dyed hair was turning grey. He said he was feeling his age but that was about all he could feel. The rest of him was numb. Soon I was virtually having to drag him into the bedroom. Jackie caught him asleep in the shop one day, completely knackered. Eventually I confessed that all this nookie was because I wanted another baby but Ron said we should slow down a bit and talk things over. I thought about taking him in for an MOT.

'DD was still hovering around like a vulture – a favourite hobby of hers. At Mike's graduation ceremony, she insisted on having a photo taken of Mike holding Josh. I knew what she was getting at. You wouldn't mind but she even wore the same hat as me. Trying to dress young to win Ron back, it was pathetic. But I felt really left out that day. DD seemed intent on playing happy families. I thought if I wasn't going to be Mrs. Bun-in-the-oven, the shopkeeper's pregnant wife, I could keep Ron with a piece of paper. So on the spur of the moment, I asked him to marry me. I said it was partly so we could get Josh christened. Ron pointed out that he wasn't divorced from DD yet but he agreed to go ahead with the christening anyway. I thought at least it was a step in the right direction.

'I still reckon I could've pulled it off – even with Mike as Josh's godfather, would you believe – if only I hadn't lost me rag. But Ron's daughter Jacqui overheard me blasting off to Jackie Corkhill about Ron arranging the godparents and he wasn't even Josh's father. Me and my big mouth. Jacqui never has liked me. She reckons I split Ron and DD up but their marriage was washed out anyway. I pleaded with Jacqui not to tell Ron but she wasn't having it. She made me tell him. Talk about hitting the fan...

'To say Ron wasn't happy is like saying Barbara Cartland is quite fond of pink. He stormed out of the flat, taking his precious records with him. He forgot one – his Benny Hill LP. When he asked for it back, I told him he could whistle for it. I caught him round at Jackie Corkhill's and thought he was shacked up with her. I was so angry I tipped pot noodle all over his head. It wouldn't have been so bad, but he hates pot noodle. I thought I'd lost him for good, particularly when I cut up all his clothes. Still at least I didn't go as far as that Bobbit woman. Of course, DD was loving every minute of it. She reckoned she was getting Ron back and arranged for them to have their marriage vows renewed. Me and Josh were all set to leave for London – there seemed nothing left for us in Liverpool – but I realised I couldn't just walk away from Ron like that. Fortunately, he felt the same and abandoned DD

half-way through the service. It was sad really – all those vol-au-vents going to waste.

'So it all worked out for me in the end. Ron accepted Josh as his own son and Mike was happy not to have the responsibility. And DD? Who cares what she thinks?'

I was all set to take Josh to London – but Ron stopped me just in time.

THE BROOKSIDE FILES

Eddie Banks on His Relationship With His Daughter-in-Law Sarah

As he and Rosie began to drift apart, Eddie Banks found himself spending more and more time with his daughter-in-law Sarah. They enjoyed each other's company. Then one night, they ended up sleeping together in her flat. This is how Eddie remembers the bizarre love tangle.

'I'd always liked Sarah. She was a smashing girl. If the truth be told, she was too good for our Carl. Rose and her didn't get on though. You know what mothers are like protecting their sons, and when Becca came along, Rose became the interfering grandmother. Whatever Sarah did was wrong as far as Rosie was concerned. I usually ended up acting as referee, trying to keep the two of them apart. In fact, I tended to sympathise more with Sarah, but it was never a good idea to tell Rosie you thought she was in the wrong – not unless you fancied sleeping on the sofa.

'Not that it would have mattered much last year, because after losing the baby and then having the hysterectomy, Rose didn't want me anywhere near her. Part of it was cos she blamed me for telling the doctor to go ahead with the operation. I was only trying to do what was best for her health, but she didn't see it that way.

'Then of course came the gambling. She started spending more time at bingo than with me. I hardly ever saw her – I felt like we were leading separate lives. Our Carl had just gone off to Dubai and I knew Sarah and Becca would be at a loose end so one evening when Rose had abandoned me again in search of a full house, I called round with a takeaway. We had a good time. It was nice to be able to talk to Sarah without Rose putting her spoke in all the time. We didn't feel we were on trial. A week or so later, Sarah invited us both round for a meal, but Rose preferred to go to her damn bingo. I thought it was disgusting that she would rather go to bingo than spend time with her family, but it was water off a duck's back. I wasn't going to turn down the offer of a free meal, so I went round on me tod. It was smashing having someone to talk to, someone who wasn't obsessed with winning money. Hadn't we already

Mal Young: 'The relationship between Eddie Banks and his daughter-in-law, Sarah, started because the writers saw a natural attraction on screen between the two. It wasn't actually planned – it just happened. And because it came out of the characters, it felt right. It was also interesting to show a guy in his forties making a fool of himself. For her part, Sarah was vulnerable and Eddie exploited the opportunity. We were happy to be seen as condemning the relationship. Neither person gained anything from it. Eddie was left no better off and in the end had to crawl back to Rosie.'

SEX

I was scared Sarah would go back to our Carl.

won enough on the lottery? Sarah and I realised we had a lot in common. We were both feeling a bit lonely and neglected and I think chatting things over – about relationships and where they go wrong – helped cheer us both up. It certainly did me a power of good.

'God knows, I needed a sympathetic ear over the next couple of months. Things at home were getting steadily worse. Rose just could not – would not – accept that she had a problem. When I found out how much she'd been spending, that she'd gambled away our holiday, I couldn't bear to be under the same roof as her. I asked Sarah if I could stay over and she let me sleep on the couch. She offered to have a word with Rosie for me but all she got for her trouble was a mouthful of abuse.

'The final straw was when Rose admitted that it was she, not Lee, who had been stealing from Grants. How could she have put our son through that, particularly after all his previous problems with the law? That was it. I'd had enough and started packing.

'Sarah let me stay at her flat. I found myself increasingly drawn to her but I hadn't realised how much until she told me she was thinking about going out to Dubai to make a fresh start with Carl. I immediately began putting all sorts of obstacles in the way. It dawned on me that I was

Rosie's gambling madness pushed me into Sarah's arms.

jealous. It got worse when Terry Sullivan started sniffing around. He clearly fancied Sarah but I didn't want him coming between me and her. I began acting like the heavy father-in-law, warning her to be careful of men like Terry and reminding her that she was still married. Understandably, she got annoyed. I felt rotten – I thought I'd blown it.

'The following night, Sarah was going to Sinbad's party. I gave it a miss in case I bumped into Rosie, but I was dead jealous when Terry came to collect Sarah. My feelings for her were eating me up. I wanted to come clean and tell her how I felt so when she got back we had a heart-to-heart. I admitted how jealous I was seeing her with other men. I thought she'd be furious but she said she was flattered. I couldn't believe that a pretty girl like her would be attracted to a big lump like me, but it seemed she was. I leaned over to kiss her and she responded. After that, one thing led to another and we ended up in bed.

SEX

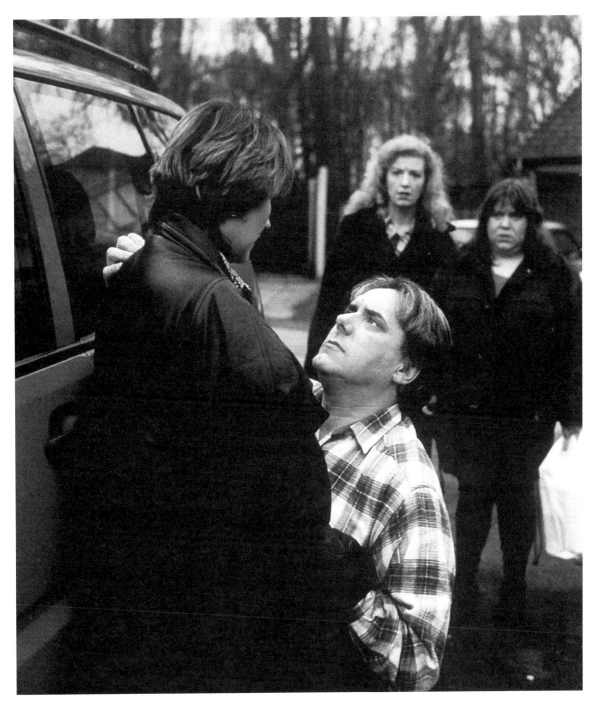

*I made a right fool of meself when Sarah left –
in front of Rosie too.*

THE BROOKSIDE FILES

'In the morning we were both in a state of shock. I thought I'd better leave. I told her that the sex was fantastic but I could no longer trust myself to be in the same room as her. She said there was no need for me to move out – it was as much her fault as mine and she'd make sure there was no repeat performance. We just had to put it behind us and pretend it had never happened.

'That was easier said than done. The temptation was just too great. Somehow the fact that we were sort-of-related didn't matter. On the contrary, it felt so right. I tried it on again a few nights later, but this time Sarah pushed me away. And to make sure I didn't climb into the wrong bed in future, she took Becca in to sleep with her. Sarah said what we had done was immoral. Deep down, I had to admit it was a bit out of order, but I couldn't help the way I felt. Sarah was made of stronger stuff than me though – either that or she didn't fancy me as much as I fancied her. She started keeping me at arm's length and tried to get me and Rosie back together. But I didn't want Rosie any more. I wanted Sarah. When Rosie tried to get me to go back home, I blurted out that I couldn't because I was in love with another woman.

'Sarah went spare when she found out what I'd told Rosie. She laid down the law in no uncertain terms. What happened between us was a mistake, she said – we had no future together. Still I thought I could talk her round. I had a word with Ron Dixon about being with a younger woman and he told me that love conquers all, regardless of any local gossip. Then again, Ron hadn't slept with his daughter-in-law. Julia Brogan would have a field day with that one!

'I went back to have another talk with Sarah. Couldn't she see how much I cared for her? She just looked me straight in the eye and told me she was disgusted and ashamed by our sleeping together and never wanted to see me again. I was a broken man.

'I spent the night outside her flat, hoping against hope for another chance, but she made it clear she didn't want to see me. I had no option but to swallow my pride and go back to Rosie. She was really trying hard to get things back to normal but my mind and my heart were still with Sarah. Eventually I couldn't stand it any longer and went round to the pizza parlour where Sarah worked and told her that I loved her. I wanted to leave Rosie and make a fresh start with Sarah. To hell with wagging tongues! I knew we could make a go of it. I knew we'd be happy together. But she wasn't interested and had already made her decision to go back to live with her parents down south. I'd lost her.

'I was too upset to say goodbye, but Sarah ordered the taxi to stop on the Close. Why did she do that if she didn't love me? I tried to keep calm but in the end I just broke down sobbing at her feet, telling her over and over how much I loved her and wanted to be with her. What I didn't know was that Rosie and Mo were standing just a few yards away and had heard everything.

'That took some sorting out, I can tell you. But we decided to call it quits – an eye for an eye. Her gambling and my affair. The saddest thing of all is that we don't get to see Becca. Sarah won't let me anywhere near her and Rose wants absolutely nothing to do with Sarah. It's the same old story. The only ones who suffer in these crazy affairs are the children.'

SEX

Lindsey Stanlow on Husband Gary and Mike Dixon

Lindsey Stanlow was put in an impossible position by husband Gary. He said that he would only go to the police and say he planted the drugs in daughter Kylie's teddy bear if Lindsey agreed to go back and live with him. Knowing that Gary's evidence was the only chance of freeing boyfriend Mike Dixon from jail in Bangkok, she reluctantly consented. But, as she recalls, that was just the start of her problems.

Having to go back to Gary tore me apart. But I knew there was no other way of freeing Mike and, as Gary was all too quick to point out, it was both our faults that Mike was in prison. You can't imagine my emotions when I heard that Mike was coming home. On the one hand, I was overjoyed but on the other I was so sad that I wouldn't be there to greet him. During those weeks in that awful hell-hole, all he had to cling to was the hope that one day he'd be reunited with me. And when that day finally came, where was I? With my husband, the man responsible for him being in jail in the first place. I knew Mike would be inconsolable, and who could blame him?

'Soon after, Mike came round to find out whether I really had done a deal with

Mal Young: 'We'd seen Jimmy's daughter, Lindsey, a few years ago and she had proved a very popular character. We thought she worked really well on screen but then Claire Sweeney, the actress who plays her, became unavailable. She's a singer and dancer who tours the world and was away for long periods. But during that time we developed Jimmy and Jackie as a family unit and it became so successful that we wanted to go back in time and look at their history. We thought that Jimmy would now want his family together. As fate would have it, at the same time as we were planning this, Claire Sweeney wrote to me saying: "I'm back in Liverpool. I'm free. Is there any chance of Lindsey ever appearing again?" So we had a ready-made character with a history. We looked back into our Brookside bible and saw that Jimmy hadn't been allowed to go to her wedding to Gary, and we had never met Gary. And of course we had this great on-going feud between the Dixons and the Corkhills, our own Montagues and Capulets. It was like the Mafia where sons and daughters of opposing gangs marry to bring the families together – and that would be Mike and Lindsey. It felt natural for them to fall in love, but we wanted the theme of drugs to keep coming back and wreak havoc on these two families. There were a few high-profile cases of young people being caught with drugs and suddenly facing the death penalty in Bangkok. On the face of it, when you read the papers, they were just normal kids. We wanted to see what would happen if some of our normal kids went through an experience like that and Ron and Jimmy had to come together to get them out, all the while hating each other.'

Gary. I said it was true. He understood my motives and we started to kiss, just like before. Then Gary walked in and Mike went for him. I thought he was going to kill him. The last thing I wanted was for Mike to end up back in jail. He wanted me to leave with him but Gary, battered and bruised, reminded me that I had sworn to stay, on Kylie's life. Besides, I knew that if I did go off with Mike, Gary would only cause more trouble. He was so eaten up with jealousy that wherever we went, he'd find us. And we'd already seen what he was capable

Gary turned nasty when I tried to avoid having sex with him. He told me I'd broken our agreement.

of. In the circumstances, I felt I had no choice but to stay. I was trapped and Gary was holding the keys.

'I was sure I'd lost Mike for good – I heard he was seeing other girls. Meanwhile Gary was playing happy families, pretending everything in the garden was rosy. But I still couldn't let him touch me. When he began to get frustrated and annoyed, I tried to calm him down by telling him I

SEX

needed time to readjust. The truth was, the only person I wanted to sleep with was Mike.

'Mum could see our marriage was a sham and did her best to persuade me to leave Gary, but I couldn't. Then one morning, Gary came home after working nights on the cabs. He brought me a bunch of flowers, a box of chocolates and breakfast in bed. He was obviously trying hard, but I wasn't interested. My thoughts were with Mike. That afternoon, Gary started getting amorous and suggested I join him in bed. I pulled away, saying I had to collect Kylie soon from nursery, but he wouldn't take no for an answer. He angrily reminded me that I'd promised him we'd try for another baby, to cement our relationship. I'd never seen him like that – there was real menace in his voice. I was frightened and tried to push him off, but he pinned me down and raped me.

'When he got off and went to the bathroom, I just lay there dazed. He had destroyed what little self-esteem I had left. I had hit rock bottom. A few minutes later, I heard him go out to fetch Kylie and decided to make a run for it, to my mum's. On the way out, I looked in the mirror. There were horrible, ugly bruises all over my body and my lip was bleeding. Mum took me in and demanded to

know what had happened. Eventually I told her. Just then Gary turned up, pretending that I'd had a fall. But mum knew the truth and things got really nasty. She threatened to go to the police, but he just laughed in her face. How could it be rape, he argued, when I was his wife? He said he wanted me back ... or else. I was so confused I didn't know what to do for the best. The only thing I did know was I didn't want Mike to find out what Gary had done to me.

Deep down I knew that Mike was still the only man I wanted.

THE BROOKSIDE FILES

'Mum managed to get a local gangster, Big Davey, to put the frighteners on Gary. She told him that Gary had been talking to the police about drug trafficking from Holland, that Gary had stitched Davey up. Gary was on the run, a frightened man. He made one last effort to take me with him – it was our fifth anniversary – but I finally summoned up the courage to tell him to get lost.

'Getting rid of Gary was all very well, but I was no nearer making up with Mike. In fact, he was all set to embark on a new life in America. Fortunately his dad had a change of heart about me, a Corkhill, and, with a little help from my mum, engineered a farewell party for Mike at La Luz to which I was the only other person invited. Mike and I felt dead awkward thrust together again like that. But soon the hesitation vanished and we got to talking about Bangkok and how we felt about each other. I realised that he still loved me. We left the club and went for a quiet walk. It was how I'd always dreamed it would be, when I was locked in that dark cell in Thailand, even when I was with Gary.

'Over the next few days, we grew closer and closer, eagerly making up for lost time, striving to restore our relationship to the way it had been when we set off for Australia what seemed like years ago. I was so pleased when Mike told me he was abandoning his plans to go to America. The only cloud on the horizon was sex – Mike didn't seem interested. But that all changed when we went for a day out and ended up at the sand dunes. I asked him whether he still wanted me physically and he explained that the only reason he'd been treading carefully was because he'd found out that I'd been raped. I assured him that

what Gary did to me hadn't turned me into a man-hater...and then I proved it to him, right there on the beach. It was magic and afterwards he showed me a note he had written to me in prison, but which hadn't reached me before my release. I filled up when I read: "If we ever get out of this place safely, I want you to marry me." I accepted on the spot. It was the happiest day of my life.

'Our first engagement present was to have each other's names tattooed in hearts on our ankles. It was something permanent – and that symbolised our love. We thought that with no sign of Gary, we'd have to wait five years before we could get married legally but we were determined to go ahead with an engagement party. The evening turned into a typical slanging match between our two families. After all we'd been through, Mike and I hadn't got any time for the bitching and back-biting so, using money Mr. Dixon gave us, we announced that we were going to America to get away from it all.

'We had a fabulous month away in America, and best of all, we did manage to get married, well not exactly legally... The ceremony was conducted by an Elvis Presley lookalike in Las Vegas. It was certainly different from your average register office and it meant just as much to us.

'The important thing for us now is to forget the past and look to the future. I'm all too aware of other couples who have split up after going through traumatic experiences such as ours, and I don't want it to happen to us. It worries me sometimes that Mike still seems obsessed with Bangkok. I just want us to lead a normal life and to be able to save up for a place of our own, preferably one far enough away from our feuding families. That's not much to ask from life, is it?'

WORK

Jacqui Dixon on Being a Young Entrepreneur

Jacqui Dixon is very much the ambitious young businesswoman. In 18 months, she has risen from organising car boot sales to running her own hair salon, Jacqui D's Style House. And she hasn't been afraid to step on a few toes on the way. Here she traces her meteoric rise.

'Even when I was at junior school, I had loads of plans. Like most girls of seven or eight, I wanted to be a model, star in the movies or run a chain of beauty parlours – a glamorous career where I could sip champagne and be driven off into the sunset by a handsome fella in a white tuxedo and a Ferrari. But whereas a lot of the others in my class would end up on the till at Woolies – and that's if they were lucky – I knew I had the brains and the energy to make my dreams come true.

'One thing I've never lacked is confidence. I think if you want something, you should go for it. Look at dad. I know the Moby wasn't exactly Harrod's, but it was his own business, something he had created. And he made enough from it to be able to buy his own shop and home in the end. I'm proud of him. But you have to be hard to succeed in business. The likes of Julia

Mal Young: 'Alexandra Fletcher, who plays Jacqui, first came to us as a young teenager, as did Diane Burke who plays Katie. Sometimes you think of them as still kids but you don't realise they're growing up in front of you and are coming up to their 20s. So Jacqui's development into a young businesswoman was part of seeing Alex growing up. Her playing style was always very sparky and outspoken so it felt likely that she would look after herself and get out there and not want her dad to help her. Having said that, she's definitely Ron's daughter. She's learnt a lot from her dad – she says what she thinks and doesn't like to be pushed around. We put the three girls – Jacqui, Katie and Rachel – in the bungalow to see how they'd cope living away from home, paying bills, but with dad living only two doors away. The other thing about Jacqui is that she breaks the stereotype of kids in dramas. All too often they're portrayed as down and outs and no-hopers. But there are many who are positive and successful – there's a lot of young entrepreneurs out there. Jacqui sees herself very much as a child of Thatcher.'

Peter – a lovely guy but a soft touch

Brogan used to say dad was tight-fisted because he wouldn't let her have a discount but if he'd done favours for every friend or neighbour who'd asked, he'd have soon gone bust.

'I started out as I meant to continue...with no room for sentiment. Dad wasn't too pleased when I staged the car boot sale on Brookside Parade – he was worried the competition would affect his takings – but I bet he'd have done the same if he'd been in my shoes. Another thing I learned quickly was the art of delegation. I had Lee Banks and Leo Johnson cleaning cars on the Parade (naturally I took 25 per cent commission) and got Katie to do some running around for me. Of course, she started whining that I was using her and taking advantage of our friendship, but it was just sound business practice. That's the trouble with Katie. She's a lovely girl and still my

WORK

best friend, but she can be too soft for her own good and all too easily led – and we all know what sort of trouble that's got her into in the past. But me, I'm a natural born leader.

'I didn't care when I got the sack from the leisure centre because I'd already decided I wanted to be me own boss. I'd had enough of working for other people. Why should they make money out of my hard work and initiative? Running aerobics classes and car boot sales was all very well, but I really wanted to expand into premises of my own. I'd always liked the look of the hairdressing salon on the Parade. It used to do a good trade with a decent core of customers – plenty of old dears coming in for their perms as well as young people wanting something

different. So I asked Max Farnham, who was the acting landlord in Barry Grant's absence, whether I'd be able to rent the place. He sneered at me as if I was just a kid and suggested I stick to car boot sales. I thought, I'll show him, the toffee-nosed pillock.

'As time went by and Max still had no takers, I tried again. He was a bit more approachable but still said I needed to come up with a £2,000 deposit plus three months' advance rent. I couldn't afford it. I asked Mike's boss, Shaun Brooks, to loan me the money. He was going out with Katie at the time but I could see he

---

Bev, Katie and Rachel made great models.
A pity Sammy spoiled the day.

fancied me as well. He implied that he'd lend me the money if I slept with him. I didn't like the sound of cheating on me best mate but I really needed that money. But after he'd got what he wanted, he tried to go back on his word. I wasn't having that so I "borrowed" a valuable corporate video tape he was working on and said he could only have it back if he let me have the loan. Eventually he agreed and I got the money. Unfortunately Katie found out about me and Shaun, and Mike lost his job. I was sorry that I'd hurt them, but I suppose there are always casualties in business.

'Max Farnham was gobsmacked when I came up with the readies, but wouldn't make a decision till I came up with a suitable business plan. On holiday, I met a guy called Peter Phelan, who wanted to run his own hair salon, so back in Liverpool we put our heads together and produced a business plan. Max was impressed and we were all set to open when that Dil Parmar bloke was installed as the new landlord. He said he had his own ideas for the salon. We could see it all slipping away but luckily Dil liked our enthusiasm and gave us the go-ahead. On 25 August 1995, Jacqui D's Style House was up and running.

'Peter's a good man to have around. The customers love him and he's a really good hairdresser. The only trouble is, he's got a heart of gold – he'll fall for any old sob story. First thing he did was appoint Julia Brogan, of all people, as our receptionist. Hair salons are supposed to be relaxing places but by the time customers had heard her monologue about her ailments and who was doing what with whom, they were exhausted. In one week, I had three fall asleep in the chair.

'The salon's gone from strength to strength, particularly now we've got the beauty parlour upstairs. In the summer we entered the Hair Fayre North West with Bev, Rachel and Katie as models. I managed to persuade Max Farnham into sponsoring us. He wasn't happy that the Grants logo on our stall was a bit on the small side, but by then it was too late for him to do anything about it. He should have checked these things out before parting with his money. And he calls himself a businessman! Things were going really well until Katie's drunken sister Sammy turned up, looking like she needed the mother of all makeovers. She then proceeded to announce in front of everyone that she was pregnant...and that Max was the father. I didn't know which way to look.

'You wouldn't mind, but Sammy's working for me now. She was taken on in the beauty parlour by Peter's sister Fee who manages it for me. I could murder that family sometimes. Katie helps out as well from time to time although she's still set on a career as a dancer. All I really need – apart from a rich fella – is my own house. I tried to buy number nine, but the Simpsons outbid me. It's all right living in the bungalow with the girls, but I can't help thinking I need something bigger, more appropriate. Somewhere I could entertain important business contacts without having to worry about Rachel's tights or Katie's undies being strewn across the hallway.

'All in all, I haven't done badly in 18 months. I'm still waiting to meet the fella in the tuxedo and the Ferrari and I know that Brookside Parade isn't exactly St. Tropez, but who knows, maybe tomorrow Richard Gere will walk into Jacqui D's and ask for a cut and blow dry. Now he might qualify for a discount ...'

WORK

Max Farnham on Running a Restaurant

In the two years since it opened, Grants restaurant has become established as one of the premier eating establishments on Merseyside. Proprietor Max Farnham recalls that the road to culinary acclaim has not always been smooth.

'When people come to dine at Grants, I like them to go away not only with the feeling that they have just experienced the best meal of their life, but also that the restaurant is a highly efficient, smooth-running machine. It is true that since our award from Mersey Nite Out I have become something of a local celebrity – a character, even – but I have no desire to indulge in the sort of theatricals beloved by some restaurateurs the moment they get their first Michelin star. No, I like to think that mine is a courteous, knowledgeable yet understated presence.

'However anyone who thinks that running a restaurant is a piece of cake – if you'll pardon the metaphor – is sorely mistaken. I don't mind admitting that we have had our moments of crisis, the majority caused by the regular vanishing acts of my erstwhile partner Barry Grant. I can't pretend that Barry was ever my ideal choice of business associate. He was unreliable, had a somewhat dubious reputation and, frankly, a

Mal Young: 'When Max first came in, we always said that he worked to live, not lived to work. If he could take the day off, he would. We saw him go through a young mid-life crisis and give up his job as a quantity surveyor. He's never really had much direction in his life. From the moment he left university and married Susannah, he's always been embroiled in relationships. He's never had time to think what he really wants to do. He fell into a job that was reasonably well paid but was easy. He could slope off at four in the afternoon if he felt like it. When life with Patricia started to even out a few years ago, he had more time on his hands and more money was coming in. Then Barry's influence came along – the want, want, want attitude. Barry, seeing another mug with money, pulled Max towards him and Max in turn was a bit in awe of Barry. Now that he owns the restaurant, we've seen Max become quite strong-willed, as you tend to be with your own business. He no longer suffers fools gladly – he wasn't prepared to put up with any nonsense when Rosie Banks was stealing food from him. With the exception of the houses on the Close which really exist, most of our regular locations – Brookside Parade, hospitals, flats, police stations, courtrooms, schools – are all part of the building where Mersey Television is based. It is so much more convenient and economical to film at our base. There are no restrictions and, with clever design, it is amazing how versatile our building, itself a former further education college, can become. Grants is actually our canteen. So a by-product of Max becoming a restaurateur was that our staff canteen was given a whole new facelift and had another layer added to it. Now every day we have lunch in Grants restaurant!'

THE BROOKSIDE FILES

Lily Savage and Loyd Grossman made an unusual double act for our grand opening.

knowledge of food which rarely rose above the basic. He was very much the prawn cocktail to my pate de foie gras.

'He spelt trouble from the word go. For a start, there was his curious, dare I say unnatural, relationship with Terry Sullivan. No sooner had we opened than the police had to be called in because Terry was wandering around the kitchen like a madman. God knows what the Good Food Guide would have said if he'd taken an axe to one of our diners.

'Before long, Barry's involvement in the day-to-day running of the restaurant became minimal, but he would keep interfering over staffing. He seemed quite happy to let anyone a bit down on their luck work for us. At one stage, it seemed that virtually everybody on the Close was employed by Grants in some capacity. We only needed Jimmy Corkhill and Ron Dixon for the set. We even had Beth Jordache as a waitress. Still at least her family were handy with kitchen knives. I got so fed up with Barry that I began

actively looking for a way to buy him out. However, I thought it was probably best if negotiations were conducted in a clandestine manner. Barry could be very volatile. A friend of mine from Round Table was interested in both the restaurant and Patricia's aunt, Penny Crosbie, but Barry advised Sam that it was not a good idea – not unless Sam wanted to end up as part of the foundations for a new bridge over the M62. Barry didn't frighten me, of course, although he did have the effrontery to demote me to junior partner on account of my alleged treachery.

'Then, less than six months after our opening, Barry upped and left for Florida and hasn't been seen since. How irresponsible can you get! As usual, I was left to pick up the pieces. I later discovered that Barry was up to his eyes in debt. I was seriously worried that the restaurant might go bankrupt. I'm not one who is prone to panic but we could have lost everything. And all Patricia was bothered about was that interminable campaign to free the Jordache women. I told her that I thought her priorities should lie a little closer to home.

'In the end, Patricia and I decided to buy out Barry when he gave us first refusal on his share of the restaurant, so that we could become sole owners. I went to see the bank manager, cap in hand, but all he could offer was a pittance. I get enough rubbish mail from the bank offering me loans when I don't want one, but when I do need their help, they don't want to know. So much for helping the small businessman! We were getting a bit desperate so I decided to tap the in-laws for

WORK

a loan. They took a bit of persuading but eventually David came up trumps. He could obviously see what a sound investment Grants, and indeed myself, were.

'I was very upset when Patricia left with the children. She was my rock. Now all I had left was the restaurant. But I was determined to prove that even if I couldn't make my marriages work, I could make a success of my business. I had hoped that my break-up with Patricia wouldn't affect the restaurant, but then out of the blue David demanded his loan back – in full. He said that he had lent me the money as an investment for Patricia and the children, but with them no longer featuring in the marital equation, he wished to recoup his outlay. God, that man can be so pompous sometimes! He'd lent me thousands – there was no way I could pay it back just like that. Susannah tried to sweet-talk him, but that only made matters worse. I think it was partly the fact

that she was working at the restaurant that prompted his sudden outburst.

'With more overheads than the National Grid, my only hope was to persuade David to accept a part share in the restaurant, on the understanding that he was strictly a sleeping partner. As I should have realised, there's a better chance of Linda McCartney tucking into a 12-ounce T-bone steak than there is of David Crosbie doing anything quietly. This sleeping partner was wide awake. Once he'd got his foot under the table (in fact – all the tables!), he immediately filled the place with members of his over 55s club. I thought at least it was good for trade until he calmly informed me that all the meals were on the house – in recompense for my having cancelled the club's Christmas do, a decision which, as I explained at the time, was totally beyond my control. One has to try and improve the quality of the clientele and I felt that a business party hosted by my bank manager did more for our image than a bunch of silly old farts in paper hats singing "Rudolph the Red-Nosed Reindeer".

'I thought that once he'd gained the satisfaction of revenge, he might keep out of the way, but the following week I found him putting up posters for cheap lunches. At this rate, he'll be turning the place into a transport cafe. Something will have to be done.

'Besides parboiling David, the other thing I would like to do is change the name of the restaurant. I know Grants has acquired a reputation, but I was thinking of something a little more up-market. I rather like the sound of Farnhams...'

David Crosbie, my new business partner,
God help me...

RELEVANT ORGANISATIONS

DRUGS

Cocaine Anonymous
24 hours a day tel 0171 284 1123

Drinkline
National alcohol helpline
Mon-Fri 11.00 a.m. – 11 p.m.
London only tel 0171 332 0202
All UK tel 0345 320202
24 hour dial and listen line tel 0500 801802

Drugs in Schools Helpline
Nationwide confidential drug information service
for pupils, parents and teachers
Mon-Fri 10 a.m. – 5 p.m. tel 0345 366666

Family and Friends of Drug Users
Nationwide phone counselling service
tel 01926 887414

Institute for the Study of Drug Dependence
Excellent source of information tel 0171 928 1211

Narcotics Anonymous
Network of self-help groups
10 a.m. – 10 p.m. most days tel 0171 730 0009

National Drugs Helpline
Free, confidential, 24 hours a day tel 0800 776600

Release
Specialises in legal issues about drugs
tel 0171 729 9904
Outside office hours tel 0171 603 8654

Re-Solv
Solvent abuse Mon-Fri 9 a.m. – 5 p.m.
tel 01785 817885

RELEVANT ORGANISATIONS

CHILD ABUSE

National Society for the Prevention of Cruelty to Children (NSPCC)
42 Curtain Road
London
EC2A 3NH
tel 0800 800500

HOME ALONE

Nation Childminding Association
8 Masons Hill
Bromley
BR2 9EY
tel 0181 464 6164

Daycare Trust
Wesley House
4 Wild Court
London
WC2B 4AU
tel 0171 405 5617

National Council for One Parent Families
255 Kentish Town Road
London
NW5 2LX
tel 0171 267 1361

Local Services
Police and social services

Royal Society for the Prevention of Accidents (ROSPA)
Edgebaston Park
353 Bristol Road
Birmingham
B5 7ST
tel 0121 248 2000

THE BROOKSIDE FILES

DOWN'S SYNDROME

Down's Syndrome Association
155 Mitcham Road
London
SW17 9PG
tel 0181 682 4001
fax 0181 682 4012

Portsmouth Down's Syndrome Trust
The Sarah Duffen Centre
Belmont Street
Southsea
Hants
PO5 INA

BULIMIA AND EATING DISORDERS

Eating Disorders Association
Sackville Place
44 Magdalen Street
Norwich
Norfolk
NR3 1JU

Telephone Helplines
Mon-Fri 9 a.m. – 6.30 p.m. tel 01603 621414

Youth Helpline (18 years and under)
Mon, Tues and Wed 4-6 p.m. tel 01603 765050

Recorded Message tel 0891 615466

The Priory Centre
11 Priory Road
High Wycombe
Bucks
HP13 6SL
tel 01494 21431

Society for the Advancement of Research into Anorexia
Stanthorpe
New Pound
Wisborough Green
Billingshurst
West Sussex
RH14 0EJ

RELEVANT ORGANISATIONS

STEROIDS

Institute for the Study of Drug Dependence
Waterbridge House
32-36 Loman Street
London
SE1 0EE
tel 0171 928 1211
fax 0171 928 1771

The Sports Council
Doping Control Unit
Walkden House
3-10 Melton Street
London
NW1 2EB
tel 0171 383 5667

The Centre for Research on Drugs
and Health Behaviour
200 Seagrave Road
London
SW6 1RQ
tel 0181 846 6565
fax 0181 846 6555

LOTTERY AND GAMBLING

Gamblers Anonymous and Gam-Anon
(for family and friends of gamblers)
P.O. Box 88
London
SW10 0EU
There are 24 hour helplines throughout England,
Ireland, Scotland and Wales – see local telephone
directory or ring the central helpline number:
tel 0181 741 4181

Parents of Young Gamblers
tel 0121 443 2609

THE BROOKSIDE FILES

DOMESTIC VIOLENCE

Campaign Against Domestic Violence
tel 0171 231 0415
tel 0171 375 2680

Zero Tolerance
24 hour tel 01642 851 561

MEDICAL ACCIDENT

Action for Victims of Medical Accident
Bank Chamber
1 London Road
Forest Hill
London
SE23 3TP
tel 0181 291 2793

RESIDENTS' ASSOCIATIONS

The Federation of Private Residents'
Associations Ltd.
11 Dartmouth Street
London
SW14 9BL
tel 0171 222 0037

CULTS

INFORM
Information on religious cults
tel 0171 955 7654

Cult Information Centre
tel 0181 651 3322

RELEVANT ORGANISATIONS

HEART DISEASE

The British Heart Foundation
The Heart Research Charity
14 Fitzhardinge Street
London
WIH 4DH
tel 0171 935 0185

HYPERTROPHIC CARDIOMYOPATHY

The Cardiomyopathy Association
40 The Metro Centre
Tolpits Lane
Watford
Herts
WD1 8SB
tel 01923 249977
fax 01923 249987

MENTAL HEALTH

MIND
National Association for Mental Health
Grants House
15-19 Broadway Stratford
London
E15 4BQ

Mindinfoline, Greater London
tel 0181 522 1728
outside London
tel 0345 660163

Other Brookside Titles Available from Boxtree

☐ 07522 07652   BETH JORDACHE – THE NEW JOURNALS PB   £4.99

☐ 07522 01727   DAVID CROSBIE'S MEMOIRS PB   £4.99

☐ 07522 10513   THE EARLY YEARS PB   £7.99

☐ 185283 9546   LIFE IN THE CLOSE PB   £9.99

☐ 07522 10440   SINBAD'S SCRAPBOOK PB   £10.99

All these books are available from your local bookshop or can be ordered direct, just tick the titles you want and fill in the form below.

Price and availability may change without notice.

Please send a cheque or postal order for the value of the book (postage and packing FREE) payable to BOXTREE CASH SALES.

Send to the following address:-

BROOKSIDE
Barnicoats
PO Box 11
Falmouth
TR10 9EN

Or please debit this amount from my Access/Visa card (delete as appropriate)

Card number ☐ ☐ ☐ ☐ ☐ ☐ ☐ ☐ ☐ ☐ ☐ ☐ ☐ ☐

Expiry Date ☐ ☐ / ☐ ☐

Amount £ ....

Signature ....

Name/Delivery Address ....

....

....

Postcode ....